Into the Box of Delights

Into the Box of Delights

A History of Children's Television

ANNA HOME

BBC BOOKS

Author's Acknowledgements
I would like to thank all the people who talked
to me or answered my letters and questions;
Ursula McCulloch for doing much of the initial
research; P.R. Jackson for applying his
encyclopaedic knowledge of dates and names;
and Nicola Philippi for making sense
of the manuscript.

The following BBC Videos
have been released in conjunction with
Into the Box of Delights:

The Very Best of Watch with Mother
The Very Best of The Clangers
The Very Best of The Magic Roundabout

ISBN 0 563 36061 5

First published in 1993

Published by BBC Books,
a division of BBC Enterprises Limited,
Woodlands, 80 Wood Lane, London W12 0TT

Set in Garamond ITC by Goodfellow & Egan Ltd, Cambridge
Colour separations by Radstock Reproductions Ltd, Midsomer Norton
Colour printed by Lawrence Allen Ltd, Weston-Super-Mare
Printed and bound in Great Britain by Redwood Press Ltd, Melksham

Contents

Introduction   9

1   Early Years   15

2   Puppets and Pre-school Programmes   49

3   Story-telling and Drama   79

4   Information and Specialist Programmes   109

5   Saturday Mornings   130

6   Entertainment   141

7   Conclusion   156

Major Milestones of Children's Programmes   168

Index   172

PICTURE CREDITS

To the memory of
Molly Cox
and
Cynthia Felgate

Introduction

Television for children can be an emotive subject. People in pubs argue and bet on the names of characters in *The Magic Roundabout* and who exactly Mary, Mungo and Midge were. Girls write in to ask for repeats of serials like *Ballet Shoes* and *The Secret Garden* that their mothers remember as part of their childhood. The performance of Lulu, the *Blue Peter* elephant, in 1969 is part of the national folk memory.

When the Diamond Jubilee Festival Exhibition to commemorate the sixtieth anniversary of BBC Children's Programmes was held at the Langham Hotel in London in 1983, queues stretched down Portland Place. At the Liverpool Garden Festival, in 1984, it is estimated that over 400 000 people passed through the same exhibition.

Teachers and psychologists are forever debating the detrimental effects of television on the young and it is blamed for deteriorating reading standards and sloppy speech. In 1991, Schools Minister Michael Fallon attacked the BBC's children's programmes as 'wicked, brazen and sinister'. Yet these programmes, together with much of Independent Television's output, are regarded as setting the standards for the rest of the world.

Television is undoubtedly an important influence in children's lives, one that helps to determine their taste, attitudes and knowledge of the world. A report published in 1992 asserted that most of them acquired what knowledge they had about Aids from television. However, in professional terms, makers of children's programmes often feel overlooked and under-rewarded. It is not often that the popular press reports huge sums of money being paid to them or their presenters. Children's programmes, even well-made, high-budget dramas, are rarely seriously reviewed. It is often assumed that people go into children's television only as a stepping-stone to greater things. In fact, many people make it a lifetime career.

Children's television in the United Kingdom has grown up as part of the public service tradition which has dominated broadcasting from its beginning

Queues stretched out of the Langham Hotel and down Portland Place in London during the Diamond Jubilee Festival Exhibition to commemorate the sixtieth anniversary of BBC Children's Programmes.

in 1922 until now. In the 1990s, the whole pattern of broadcasting in this country is set to change. Consumer choice and the free market economy are to be the new guidelines. The 1990 Broadcasting Act introduces a new-style

ITV Channel 3 in which the licences to broadcast have in most cases been awarded to the highest bidder. Three of the existing ITV companies – Thames, Television South and Television South West – lost their franchises and the new companies which replace them – Carlton, Meridian and West Country Television – will primarily be publisher broadcasters. This means that, apart from regional programmes, they will commission programmes from the independent market rather than making them in-house. All companies will be bound to deliver a dividend to their shareholders, as well as payments to the Treasury commensurate with the bids they made. In many cases this will mean considerable financial strain with a consequent pressure on programme-making budgets. In addition, the new regulatory body, the Independent Television Commission (ITC), will have a much lighter touch than the old Independent Broadcasting Authority (IBA). There is also the prospect of a fifth channel although, at the time of writing, this is not being hotly contested. So far, only one bidder has emerged: Thames Television.

Cable is again being talked about as a medium-term viable alternative to BBC and ITV, and in 1996 the BBC's charter is due to be renewed amid talk of pay-TV, sponsorship and advertising. By the end of the decade, British broadcasting is likely to look very different. What impact is all this going to have on television for children? The pessimistic answer is: an adverse one. It is worth noting that the original Government White Paper on broadcasting made no reference whatsoever to children's programmes, and it took a determined lobby led by British Action for Children's Television (BACTV), the Campaign for Quality Television and the broadcasters, both individuals and companies, to get a designated number of hours for children written in as obligatory for the new Channel 3 companies.

Children's television has always been acknowledged as an important part of public service broadcasting, but, equally, a vulnerable one. It seems relatively easy to displace children's programmes in favour of sport or news. This point was tellingly made in a *Points of View* programme in 1990, when a clip of David Dimbleby apologizing for the loss of the BBC pre-school programme *Playdays* because of Mrs Thatcher's resignation as prime minister was juxtaposed with one from 1965 showing his father, Richard, apologizing for a similar incident during a Budget broadcast. It is also noticeable that many ITV companies that bid for franchises may include more children's programmes in their prospectuses than are transmitted when they win the licence. Similarly, there have always been problems with the funding of children's programmes. Because they are broadcast outside peak viewing time and do not generate the huge audiences that evening programmes do, less money is allocated to them. There has tended to be an aura of *Blue Peter* 'make and do' around children's departments and a belief by those in authority that, because children are smaller than adults, their programmes cost less. But a drama is a drama. A play for children involves the same kind of money as an adult one, sometimes even more because of child actors' limited working hours and other problems.

Audiences for children's programmes are often highly respectable. Drama series like the BBC's *Grange Hill* and Granada's *Children's Ward* win over 6 million viewers and *Newsround* an average of 4.5 million. If looked at in terms of percentages of potential child viewers *Newsround* achieves about 18 per cent of four to fifteen-year-olds and *Grange Hill* 25 per cent.

In future, daytime audiences may well become more important and competitive. Already the slot immediately before the early evening news has become a battleground. *Neighbours* is currently winning the audience for the BBC's *Six O'Clock News*. Although it is watched by a great many children, it is not a true children's programme. The position of the early evening news has had an effect on various occasions on the time-slots and duration of children's output on BBC 1. If daytime competition for ratings becomes even greater, it is possible that children's programmes could get displaced into less valuable air-time or be reduced in number.

There are people who would argue that this would be a good idea, that children watch too much television and that it is in some way corrupting them and destroying their childhood. There is an element of nostalgia in this. Somehow, in the good old days of *Muffin the Mule* and *The Flowerpot Men*, in the 1940s and 1950s, all was right with the world. But today's television, they believe, is brash, aggressive and negative. It seems that people have always had these kind of feelings, and that in those good old days Muffin was the destroyer of *Children's Hour* on radio and just as evil and subversive as today's television programmes.

There is also an element of puritanism in this attitude, the idea that if something is entertaining rather than strictly educational and informative it is bad for children. It is unlikely that such strictures would be applied to adult television, so why to children's? Surely they have as much right to entertainment and relaxation after school as their elders have after a hard day at the office.

Children's television is an obvious target for moral judgement. Clearly it should be of the highest quality, but quality in the widest sense including the occasional piece of quality rubbish as well as the whole range of other programmes. The great debate over *Teenage Mutant Hero (Ninja) Turtles* has raised many of these issues again. The popular press is only too ready to blame the series for increased aggression in the playground, children exploring dangerous tunnels and supposedly flushing terrapins down the loo. It is always too easy to make television the scapegoat for the problems of society, and it is particularly easy when children are involved.

The makers of children's programmes are responsible people, often parents themselves, who walk a tightrope in their professional lives. They know they are *in loco parentis* during the time designated for children's television. But what exactly is children's television? What are the parameters in terms of age-range and content?

The programme-makers address a potential audience of 9.6 million children aged between four and fifteen years. They know that one person's nine-year-old is more like someone else's eleven-year-old and vice versa. They have to involve, stimulate and entertain this diverse audience. They want to open up the world and illuminate it. But to what extent do these broadcasting professionals have the right to introduce subjects like sex, violence and death to children they don't know, and into households that may not want to watch? It is one of the key issues in children's broadcasting today, and one which arises most frequently in contemporary drama series like the BBC's *Grange Hill* and *Byker Grove*, Granada's *Children's Ward* and Central's *Press Gang*. All these programmes try to deal with the reality of the lives of young teenagers in a way which is both entertaining and informative. It is also, at times, disturbing to adults.

Children's television today is very different from that of the 1950s and 1960s. What will it look like by the end of the decade? Indeed, will it still exist in its present form or will it, as in many other countries, have been reduced to wall-to-wall cartoons and so-called 'family drama'?

CHAPTER ONE

Early Years

One of the original commitments when John (later Lord) Reith became General Manager of the BBC in 1922 was to children. *Children's Hour* on radio was one of the earliest programmes, first broadcast in 1922, and became one of the best loved. Presenters like Uncles Caractacus (Cecil Lewis) in the 1920s and Mac (Derek McCulloch) from 1930 to 1951 and Aunties Cyclone, later Kathleen (Kathleen Garscadden) from 1924 to 1960 and Elizabeth (May Jenkin) from 1929 to 1951 were household names. Television had no committed children's hour before the Second World War, but programmes of interest to children were shown. It was a Mickey Mouse cartoon that was stopped in mid-stream when the television service closed down for the war in September 1939 – and the same cartoon re-opened the service in June 1946.

Alexandra Palace in north London, the headquarters of BBC Television, must have been a very exciting place in which to work in those days when the service started coming back to life. There were only eight production offices to cover all types of programmes and everybody did everything.

In the 1946 staff list there were two series producers and sixteen producers for the entire television service. In 1991, there were nearer 400 producers and the Children's Department alone had thirty-six.

In 1946, the person responsible for what children's programmes there were was Mary Adams, Head of Talks, Television. Her main job was to take care of adult talks programmes but she also initiated the first regular children's programme. It was transmitted live on Sunday afternoons and was variously called *For The Children* and *Children's Hour*. This confusion between titles continued until 1950. This memo from Richmond Postgate, Acting Head of Children's Programmes, is dated July 1950:

> May we please expunge the phrase 'Children's Hour'. The phrase in the *Radio Times* is 'For the Children' and the programmes themselves

might well be referred to as 'programmes for the children' or 'the children's programmes'.

It was on *For The Children* that Muffin the Mule made his first television appearance on 30 October 1946. Annette Mills, his 'co-star', had already made him famous through his appearances with the Hogarth puppets in the theatre, and he seems to have made a fairly easy transition to television where he remained a firm favourite until 1957. In January 1947, a thirteen-year-old Petula Clark appeared in her own show. Larry the Lamb, star of *Toytown*, who had been a huge success on radio, made an early transition to television in 1950 in a televised version of a stage show. *Toytown* appeared again in the mid-1950s in a puppet version produced by Gordon Murray. *For The Children* had varying time-slots and lengths in those early years. Many of the early programmes were transmitted on Sunday afternoons, which caused some anxiety in ecclesiastical circles. There was a fear that children might be seduced away from Sunday School by this exciting new medium.

Even in the very early years, a number of people were pressing for the expansion of children's programmes. In July 1947, Cecil McGivern, then Television Programme Director, wrote:

Children are fascinated by Television. The correspondence protesting against children being lured away from Sunday School by Television testifies to this... The question of a special programme for children must be tackled one day. I think we should start on it now. The present Sunday afternoon attempt at children's items is rather vague and sloppy and is just nibbling at the problem. In any case, I think we shall be very soon (because of the Sunday School controversy) be forced to make a definite statement and I think we should anticipate the matter.

At this time Mary Adams gave considerable thought to the ways in which the service for children could be expanded. They included many ideas which were subsequently developed, for instance, as this memo of 8 August 1947 shows, story-telling:

I believe story-telling (or even reading) good stories would hold interest without much additional visual support. Before the war, Lydia Lopokova used to do so with Russian folk tales, and Paul Leyssac with Hans Andersen's stories. We could simply show the illustrations while reading books like *Stuart Little* or *Babar* or *Orlando*. Or we could commission original picture stories by someone prepared to put in the necessary work.

Many of these stories did appear on children's television over the years.

Mary Adams also suggested that there should be current affairs programmes:

A children's newspaper might begin in a modest way (the sort of thing King Hall used to do). Here could appear personalities of the week as well as illustrated guides to topical events, e.g. the Budget, India, Unesco's Amazon expedition, etc.

The aim to provide current affairs programmes was translated into *Children's Newsreel* in 1950 and later, in 1972, into *John Craven's Newsround*. Some of the suggestions sound a bit heavy-handed and educational in today's terms. To quote Mary Adams again:

There should be a film in every afternoon's programme, and someone should be detailed to search ardently for suitable shorts like Secrets of Nature, How the Telephone Works, Instruments of the Orchestra, etc.

Some ideas certainly would not find favour now. For instance, it was proposed that on Sunday 23 November 1947 there should be a programme of children's music lasting about forty-five minutes and presented by Sir Malcolm Sargent. There is no way in which today's audience would be prepared to sit down and watch an orchestral programme of this nature, introduced by a pillar of the establishment and lasting for forty-five minutes. Music is extremely difficult to present on television and its straight presentation is not particularly attractive to a young audience.

Eventually, in 1948, the Director-General, Sir William Haley, agreed to the expansion of the children's service. There were the usual requests for extra staff and budgets. In fact, the whole project did not finally come to fruition until 1950 when jobs as producers in children's television were advertised. One hundred people were interviewed and seven were successful. They were Peter Thompson, Joy Harington, Dorothea Brooking, Rex Tucker, Michael Westmore, Naomi Capon and Pamela Brown. They came from a variety of backgrounds. Obviously, the main source of recruitment within the BBC, then and for many years to come, was radio.

Dorothea Brooking was a studio manager, a sound technician in radio, when she moved to television. Previously she had been an actress in Ireland.

Joy Harington had been an actress and had gone to Hollywood as a dialogue director. She coached Elizabeth Taylor for her role in *National Velvet*. She happened to hear Cecil McGivern giving a radio talk about the future of television and wrote and asked if she could be a producer. She started her television career as a stage manager, prompting actors at

Meet The Penguins: producer Dorothea Brooking with artist Bill Hooper. (BBC, 1952)

Freda Lingstrom (Head of Children's Programmes, BBC TV 1951–56) with Porterhouse the Parrot from *Saturday Special*. (BBC, 1951)

rehearsal. Her first directing experience came when the director did not turn up for some reason and sent a message to say she would have to take over. She did not even know the whereabouts of the production gallery where the producer and production staff sit.

Pamela Brown also had a theatrical background and was a successful children's author, whose books included *The Swish of the Curtain* and *Maddy Alone*.

Michael Westmore later became Head of Children's Programmes at Associated Rediffusion. Rex Tucker was a schoolmaster turned radio producer.

Before Freda Lingstrom took over as Head of the Children's Department in 1951 and started to build the BBC Children's Television Department, there was a period of about a year during which there were two acting heads of the new department: Richmond Postgate and Cecil Madden. It was an exciting and heady period. Everybody seemed to be asked to do everything. No one had any form of television training, they learnt as they went along.

Cecil Madden was obviously a lively and much-liked man with an appetite for show business. During his short tenure, a number of new programmes started including *Whirligig*. It was billed in the *Radio Times* as 'the first Children's Variety Magazine Programme' and starred Humphrey Lestocq and Mr Turnip. At various times it featured Harry Corbett and Sooty and Rolf Harris and Willoughby, a kind of animated easel. Another new programme was *Telescope*, a magazine programme, presented by Cliff Michelmore.

Sport made an early appearance on children's television, often, one feels, as a sop to adults. For example, as a bridge into adult coverage young viewers were subjected to items on the rules of tennis. Obviously, outside broadcast effort had to be maximized but there is a feeling that children were being treated as mini adults in this context.

In May 1950, Richmond Postgate sent a memo to Seymour de Lotbinere, Head of Outside Broadcasts, which gives an idea of the range of outside broadcasts that were going into children's programmes, and how these programmes fed on, and had to co-operate with, the adult output.

Cecil Madden, one of the original BBC TV producers and Acting Head of Children's Programmes, BBC TV 1950–51.

Humphrey Lestocq chatting to Mr Turnip from *Whirligig*. (BBC, 1952)

Week 26 – 28 June. To confirm that Michael Westmore will be in charge of a cricket item at the end of this programme which will be intended to lead up to the adult outside broadcast from Lord's. The timing is at present 6 p.m. but may be 5.50 p.m. if another programme item falls out...

Week 27 – 2 July. HMS *Worcester*. I am asking Dorothea Brooking and Peter Thompson to liaise with Barrie Edgar. This is not, I hope, as clumsy as it might seem and for our part we will ensure that contrary suggestions are not made to Mr Edgar.

Week 27 – 5 July. To confirm that the children's programmes should end at approximately 5.50 p.m. with a seven-minute item about the rules of tennis... so as to lead up to the outside broadcast from Wimbledon.

Week 28 – 12 July – Holly Hill. To confirm that we would like 5.10 p.m. to 5.30 p.m. on sheep-dogs and sheep, and that Michael Westmore will liaise with your producer Berkeley Smith.

Week 30 – 23 July. Subject to decision as to the venue, we hope that Dorothea Brooking will liaise with your producer on a new and old agricultural implements programme.

Week 31 – 30 July. I am provisionally scheduling 20 minutes of air training from Castle Bromwich and will later allot a producer.

It was something of a hotch-potch, and one wonders how the children of that time took to it. On the other hand, television was such a novelty that it was all new and exciting.

In 1950, when the new producers came together, children's programmes were still based at Alexandra Palace. However, during that year, they moved to Lime Grove in Shepherds Bush in West London where they had their own studio which was blessed by the Bishop of Grantham and formally inaugurated by Mrs Attlee, wife of the prime minister, in these words:

The first *Children's Hour* ever to be televised from these studios. It's always exciting to be in at the beginning of anything new. Perhaps in

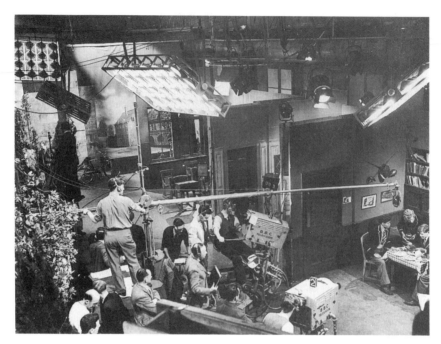

Recording of *Billy Bunter of Greyfriars School* in Studio H, Lime Grove. The studio became the home of BBC children's programmes from September 1951.

years to come you'll be telling your children how you saw the first *Children's Hour* ever to be televised from Lime Grove Studios. It gives me great pleasure to declare the new studio open.

Lime Grove was a former film studio. It was then, and remained, a warren of corridors and staircases. The lift was so slow and so small that people were forever being lost. There are also stories about various wild animals getting stuck in the lift when *Blue Peter* was there. Children's programmes were made in Lime Grove until the 1960s, often sharing uneasily with current affairs programmes. From the mid to late 1960s there was a demarcation line across the studio. Half was for current affairs and half for *Jackanory*; there were real rows if the straw for the *Jackanory* stable set happened to drift across the line or if the programme overran.

There were problems in the early 1950s as well. Precious rehearsal time was lost when actors and other performers disappeared to the canteen. There was talk about providing trolleys in Studio D for large orchestras or *corps de ballet*. There was also a severe shortage of basic equipment. Apparently the BBC's only upright piano was required in Alexandra Palace and could not be removed. History does not relate how this problem was solved.

The entire children's television output came from one studio. There were three cameras to cover the programmes plus the presentation announcer, and directors moved in and out of the chair as their programme came up. It was in conditions like this that the original productions of *The Railway Children* and *The Secret Garden* were broadcast live. There was one transmission during the week with a live repeat, often with a totally different crew, on Sundays.

In those days, the amount of telecine (film inserts) was relatively small so there was great pressure on the actors and the camera crews. In an early report on children's television in 1954, the lack of television technique on the part of actors was much stressed.

The Railway Children: (left to right) Michael Croudson (Peter), Carole Lorimer (Phyllis), Marian Chapman (Bobbie), Marjorie Manning (Mrs Perks) and Thomas Moore (Master Perks). (BBC, 1951)

Filming of *The Secret Garden* with Elizabeth Saunders who played Mary Lennox. (BBC, 1952)

Huw Wheldon introducing some Polish children on the seventy-fifth edition of
All Your Own. (BBC, 1960)

Actors were often placed in hazardous situations. Peter Hawkins, best
known perhaps for the voices of Bill and Ben 'The Flowerpot Men', tells how,
when taking part in *Aladdin* in 1951, he had to dive through an open window
and reappear on set fairly smartly. Unfortunately, nobody had removed the
washing-line that was outside the window. But they had moved the mattress
on which he was supposed to fall. He made his re-entry on time.

Cliff Michelmore first appeared on children's television in 1950 in an
outside broadcast from Wimbledon. In 1952 he became the editor of *All Your
Own.* This showed children enjoying hobbies and displaying their talents,
and was the programme on which Huw Wheldon, Managing Director, BBC
Television from 1968 to 1975, appeared as presenter. His attitude was
somewhat patrician. When he carelessly leant on a harpsichord made by a
child entirely out of matchsticks and reduced it to ruins, he remarked, 'I'm
sure you can stick it together again.'

Children's announcer Jennifer Gay with Richard Dimbleby in Calais for the first television broadcast from across the Channel. (BBC, 1950)

It is interesting that at this early stage children's programmes and, indeed, adult ones, were linked by a live presenter. From the mid-1960s on this became unfashionable as it was thought too cosy and soft. It has never really reappeared for adult television, but the live presenter was revived again in children's television at a time when the BBC was losing out badly to ITV and needed a new look. That was in 1985, when Phillip Schofield made his first appearance on BBC Children's Television.

In 1949, the presenter was a fourteen-year-old schoolgirl, Jennifer Gay, daughter of the conductor Hugo Rignold. After four years she left to continue her ballet training. There were, however, hazards in using a schoolgirl. Programme meeting minute, January 1951:

Jennifer has chicken pox. Substitutes discussed.

The output in those early days was very ambitious. In the minutes of the programme meeting of 31 October 1950 the following programmes were mentioned: a special item for Hanukkah; *Little Grey Rabbit*; *The Reluctant Dragon*; a Christmas Day party from Hammersmith Palais (which Vic Oliver later described as the hardest work he'd ever done); *Cruise of the Toytown Belle*; *The Little Fire Engine*, a new story by Graham Greene; Norman Harper and his horse Starlight (it was suggested that this act should be used at the Hammersmith Palais party or in the studio if the horse was not likely to damage the floor); *The Junior Inventors Club*; *The Black Arrow*; and toys for Christmas.

There was a discussion about Enid Blyton and Captain W.E. Johns, the author of the *Biggles* books. (In later years, Freda Lingstrom would never have permitted the thought of Enid Blyton and it was not until 1992 that Noddy hit BBC television screens.) Serialization of Enid Blyton's *Caravan Children* and Noel Streatfeild's *Ballet Shoes* was discussed. There was to be a special *Uncle Remus* programme and there was talk of teenage programmes, which came to fruition in 1953. Many other items and possible programmes were discussed.

E. Nesbit's *Five Children and It* was done for the first time in 1951. In this version, the Psammead was played by a small boy who mimed to an actor's

Five Children and It: the character of the Psammead was played by Thomas Moore. (BBC, 1951)

Five Children and It: an updated version forty years on with a new-look Psammead operated by Francis Wright. (BBC, 1991)

voice. In the 1991 version, the Psammead was a sophisticated puppet made by the BBC Special Effects Department.

Cecil Madden was clearly eager to do his utmost for the young audience, so much so that he was castigated in no uncertain terms for great extravagance. In April 1951 there was an exchange of memos between him and Cecil McGivern, Controller, Television Programmes, about fitting *Muffin the Mule* and the drama *The Black Arrow* in one studio. Cecil Madden was asking for two studios during the single transmission period. McGivern says:

This in my opinion would not only be the most dangerous precedent but considerably extravagant. In the past you yourself have on numerous occasions expressed alarm to me at the very considerable spread of sets and the increasing complications of producer, studio and scenic demands. When you were on this end of television you saw clearly the dangers of giving section heads and producers a free rein in this respect. It seems to me that you have forgotten that very right attitude and this latest request for two studios for a sixty-minute transmission period (or the decision to drop essential programme items in order to leave room for the serial) is really the most extravagant studio request which has been made.

1951 was the year of the Festival of Britain and children's television was involved in a competition for designing posters for the exhibition. As one education officer somewhat caustically remarked, it was difficult to judge the contest as the entries were shown on television in black and white and there were so many of them. Obviously, children then were just as enthusiastic about joining in as they are today.

In May 1951 Freda Lingstrom arrived to take over as Head of the Children's Department and started to build the BBC Children's Television that we know today. At first there was general resistance. The young producers thought she was likely to be much less fun and much less easygoing than Cecil Madden. It is a tribute to her that within a few weeks they were all calling her 'Mum', a title she bore to the end of her career. Others called her, less reverently, 'the old cough drop', but never to her face.

She appears to have been a formidable woman of many talents. She was an artist who held one-woman shows and was also a novelist. She cared deeply for the child audience and fought hard for them. She held very strict views about correct standards and would criticize if she thought work was shoddy or tasteless. She abhorred any hint of commercialism. The word 'Hoover' was never permitted – vacuum cleaner only. Even then, she worried that the Hoover would be recognizable by its shape. She clearly inspired respect and affection in her staff. 'Fair' is a word often used of her. She also had a generous side. When she received the OBE in 1955 she gave a party at the Gore Hotel for the whole department and each secretary received a handkerchief as a gift.

Few dared joke with her, although Humphrey Lestocq of Mr Turnip fame once did a double-take and said, 'I'm sorry, I thought you were Peter Butterworth,' (of the *Carry On* . . . films). He survived.

Freda Lingstrom is best known as the creator, together with her colleague and companion Maria Bird, of *Andy Pandy* and *The Flowerpot Men*. A huge success in their own era, these characters had a great revival as part of the *Watch with Mother* video in the late 1980s, and indeed topped the video bestseller lists. The *Watch with Mother* series, also created by Freda Lingstrom, was in itself an innovation: the first coherently planned combination of education and entertainment specifically for very small children, with each day having its own flavour.

It is noticeable that once Freda Lingstrom arrived the notes of the departmental meetings became much fuller and more formal. It is clear that she was a firm administrator. In December 1951 she told producers that the Controller, Television Programmes, Cecil McGivern, had said there would be a little more money for children's television in the New Year. However, she also asked them to observe the same austerity in their productions as they had during the last three months so that a reserve fund could be put up enabling her to be 'generous on occasions' and allow each producer in turn a 'glossy production'.

Freda Lingstrom was determined to continue the expansion of the Children's Department. She was vigorous in defending her territory and there were lively exchanges between her and Cecil McGivern.

An example is this memo to her from Cecil McGivern in September 1952:

Two points.
1.   Wednesday 24 September, *Men at Work*, (2) 'Apple Growing'.
Did you consider this suitable (from the pont of view of atmosphere, style of speech, content, etc.) for children, and did you consider this entertainment or even entertaining education?

2.   Sunday 28 September
Do you consider this programme *as a whole* suitable for children's television which is to be *entertainment*, and suitable for Sunday which is the main viewing in the week, and do you consider the first two items (migrant butterflies and printing patterns on leaves) suitable for a programme which is meant to be entertaining with education items judiciously placed in the spread. Children's television *must not* become school's television . . .

Freda Lingstrom's response is trenchant:

The short answer to both your points is 'no'. The notes attached are offered not as excuses, but as facts having some bearing on these two bad days.

1. *Men at Work*

'Apple Growing' was one of a series based on films offered by Howard Thomas and designed to show countrymen at work as opposed to the last series on factory workers in towns. The remaining ones will show a blacksmith, a baker, a basket-maker and a dairyman, all of which having much more action will be more easily presented. For this series we sought the co-operation of Midland region and then Godfrey Baseley selected countrymen he knew hoping that they would feel easy and confident with him. Baseley, himself an experienced interviewer in sound, was nervous and stilted. Smith, an expert at his job, was almost tongue-tied. The subject was too difficult and the result was what you saw. I am sorry, we hope to redeem the series quickly.

2. Sunday 28 September

When this Sunday was originally planned it was intended to include the conkers programme [*The Conker King*, actually transmitted the following month]. This, however, had to be postponed because Huw Wheldon could not as he had hoped return in time to do his part. Conkers would have added the right note but the programme as a whole failed because the ballet was totally unsuitable for children ... The ballet, well done though it was, was precious and sophisticated to a degree, even occasionally to a point of slight decadence, and I watched it with increasing dismay. It was the worst possible choice for children on Sunday or any other day. *Still under the impression that the ballet was going to be amusing* I filled in the few minutes left vacant by the conkers programme with a piece on butterflies.

The intention was that as many boys put butterflies into jars and boxes at this time of the year, under the impression that they would hibernate, a short programme with the stress on observing butterflies rather than catching and keeping them might be of value. It was certainly not intended to teach in the accepted sense of the word ... The percentage of general interest programmes is not very great, rarely more than forty minutes in a week, often only thirty. Can there be any danger of children's television becoming school's television with approximately 11/12 of it being pure entertainment?

There is another nice exchange between Cecil McGivern and Freda Lingstrom in July 1953.

FROM: Controller of Programmes, Television
SUBJECT: Names in children's television: The Appleyards! The Bastables!
TO: HCP (Tel)

Terrible names. Names should be attractive, catching on. These two sound like suet puddings with a mixture of cement.

Freda Lingstrom replies on his own memo:

The Treasure Seekers – The Bastables were invented 50 years ago [by E. Nesbit] and are loved by nearly all children who still read the book. The Appleyards seem to have caught on with a vengeance. Sylvie's report on the whole series gives an appreciation index of 85! What about Bultitude [in Anstey's *Vice Versa*] for a name anyway?

The coronation of Elizabeth II in 1953 established television as a serious alternative to radio. There were children's programmes in coronation week – and even on the day itself, when Cliff Michelmore, who had spent the previous week scouring the country for suitable children, directed fife and drum bands and various other activities live in the studio. The programme was somewhat under-rehearsed and he was unable to stop them performing. There were also rather serious programmes intended to explain the significance of monarchy to a child audience.

The 1950s were a golden age of children's television. Under Freda Lingstrom, and initially under Owen Reed who succeeded her in 1956, children's programmes thrived. The titles are still remembered. They include *All Your Own*, *The Appleyards* (a precursor of today's soaps), *Playbox*, *Picture Book*, *Billy Bunter of Greyfriars School*, *Andy Pandy* and *The Secret Garden*.

The younger members of *The Appleyard* family: (left to right) David Edwards (John), Barbara Brown (Hazel), Derek Rowe (Tommy), Erica Houen (Sally) and Carole Olver (Margaret). (BBC, 1957)

During this period many people who were to become household names in both adult and children's television were first associated with the department. Huw Wheldon and Cliff Michelmore have already been mentioned. Tony Hart was an artist and illustrator on *Saturday Special* (1952–53) and is now, after forty years' unbroken service, a presenter on *Hartbeat*. He has survived many difficult television moments and has the scars to prove it, bitten by many an animal star. Perhaps no episode was more unpleasant than the one that involved a skunk he was using as a live model in the old Dickenson Road Studio in Manchester (a converted chapel). The skunk did what skunks are prone to do, and the result left Tony struggling for breath and unable to continue the rehearsal. Leonard Chase, the producer, thought he was fooling around but, once he had descended to the studio floor, realized the situation was serious. He called for air freshener, the show went on and Tony survived – but he will never forget the occasion. Other well-known names include Peter Hawkins, an actor on *Whirligig* (1950–56) who was most recently the voice of *Penny Crayon* (1989); and Peter Butterworth, a presenter on *Saturday Special* (1951–53) who appeared in sixteen *Carry On...* films. Shaun Sutton, actor and writer/producer on *Huckleberry Finn* (1952) was Head of the BBC Drama Group from 1969 to 1981, and Sir David Attenborough, who first appeared on *Zoo Quest* in 1954, was Controller of BBC 2 from 1965 to 1968 before returning to film-making in 1972.

In 1955, ITV started broadcasting and this resulted in a completely new situation: competition. At first the new service did not appear to be much of a threat. Its coverage was not nation-wide and initially its children's programmes were relatively low key in public service mode, and did not present much of a challenge to the established BBC schedule.

However, by 1956 this situation had changed and when Owen Reed took over from Freda Lingstrom he was told by Cecil McGivern that his mission was to regain the audience without dropping standards.

ITV had initiated a policy of westerns and adventure series like *Roy Rogers*,

Royal visitors Prince Charles and Princess Anne chatting to David Attenborough and Cocky the cockatoo after seeing a recording of the magazine programme *Studio E*. (BBC, 1958)

Hopalong Cassidy, Rin Tin Tin, Lassie and *The Adventures of Robin Hood*, which was *the* great success. These series were winning hands down in children's terms. The figures were not all that clear at this stage as the ITV service still was not national, but where figures were comparable, i.e. on sets that were able to receive all channels, the figures in 1956 and 1957 were as follows:

1956	BBC:ITV
First quarter London	50:50
Second quarter London and Midland	40:60
Third quarter London, Midland and the North	34:66
Fourth quarter London, Midland and the North	26:74
1957	BBC:ITV
First quarter London, Midland and the North	28:72
Second quarter London, Midland and the North	30:70

At this period ITV was winning 3 to 1 in terms of children.

Owen Reed fought back by increasing the volume of drama and introducing series of quality, like *Champion the Wonder Horse*, bought in mainly from the United States. This policy improved the BBC's ratings although it did not solve the problem completely. Throughout the late 1950s and 1960s the pressure of competition was considerable.

The Children's Department remained very vulnerable, particularly in terms of the build-up of the early evening figures towards peak time. Owen Reed recognized the need for the department to develop and change but was hamstrung by a lack of money and resources. Increasingly, those then running the television service seemed to view a dedicated children's service as a liability rather than an asset. Indeed, in 1959, the title 'Children's Television' was dropped in the *Radio Times* and was no longer used when programmes were announced. The intention was to avoid alienating a wider public from watching these particular programmes.

The main battleground as far as the long-term future of the Children's Department was concerned was the area of drama. Traditionally, the department had provided drama both during the week and on Sundays. The

Sunday serials had always had 'family appeal' but were intended primarily for children. Now it was felt that the family audience was more important and would be better catered for by the Adult Drama Department. A new scenario for the Children's Department was drawn up which excluded drama and light entertainment. The first Sunday serial to be made under this arrangement was *Oliver Twist* in 1962. Owen Reed demanded that there should be editorial input from the Children's Department. He felt that it was a very frightening story, and was concerned that the script had been written for adults and that it was being produced by a producer who had no experience in children's programming. His request was not accepted and the programme went out with close-ups of Nancy's head being beaten in by Bill Sykes. Public reaction showed that a number of children had nightmares and Owen Reed felt that his position had been vindicated. However, things did not improve and he continued to make pleas for the reinstatement of a dedicated children's service.

This was not the intention of the men then running the television service: Stuart Hood (Controller of Programmes), Donald Baverstock (Assistant Controller, Programmes) and Kenneth Adam (Director of Television). The situation was exacerbated by personal ill-feeling between Reed and Hood. In 1963, Owen Reed was moved firmly sideways to Staff Training and Ursula Eason, his deputy, held the fort until 1964 when the Children's Department was amalgamated with Women's Programmes to form Family Programmes. Doreen Stephens was appointed head of the new department.

Doreen Stephens had been working in Women's Programmes and was not particularly enamoured of taking on a department which included children's programmes, about which she knew very little. She inherited *Watch with Mother*, the once-a-week *Blue Peter*, which was in its very early stages, a considerable amount of acquired material and the programme for deaf children. She also inherited a dispirited department shaken by the split-up, much reduced in size and short of cash and resources.

However, the advent of BBC 2 in 1964 meant a huge expansion in all kinds of programming including children's. Michael Peacock, Chief of Programmes, BBC 2, had seen the pre-school American series *Romper Room* transmitted by Anglia Television and decided that BBC 2 should have a daily pre-school

Ursula Eason, pioneer of programmes for the deaf and Assistant Head of Children's Programmes, BBC TV 1955–70.

Doreen Stephens, Head of Family Programmes, BBC TV 1964–67.

series of a similar nature but home-grown. This was the genesis of *Play School*.

It was during Doreen Stephen's regime that *Blue Peter* really became established as a national institution and another national institution, *The Magic Roundabout*, was created. Joy Whitby was the producer brought in to set up *Play School* and formed a team which went on to start the long-running story-telling programme *Jackanory* in 1965. The amalgamated department did not survive for very long and in 1967, when Doreen Stephens left the BBC together with Joy Whitby to help set up the new London Weekend Television (LWT) franchise, Huw Wheldon, then Controller of Programmes, decided that the Children's Department should be reinstated. Monica Sims was appointed its head.

Monica Sims was another reluctant recruit to Children's Television. She had been a producer in Women's Programmes in television and had then

Monica Sims, Head of Children's Programmes, BBC TV 1967–78.

moved to become editor of *Woman's Hour* on radio. She was enjoying this a great deal when Huw Wheldon persuaded her that she really should be running Children's Programmes. Once she had taken over she became totally involved and dedicated to the future of the department. Under her, it moved forward into a second golden age. She inherited the situation that had been left by Doreen Stephens. That is, drama and light entertainment programmes were still being made outside the department.

In 1969, she made a number of points about the current status and future of children's programmes in a report to the BBC's General Advisory Council:

Introduction

'How could you replace Dougal with President Nixon? It is time you got your priorities right.'

That lighthearted letter from Cambridge was one of many this year which have rebuked the BBC for allowing the pattern of children's viewing to be interrupted by events which may be important to adults but which hold no interest for children. I quote it not because of the unfortunate fact that the timing of children's programmes makes them particularly vulnerable to cancellations or curtailment as a result of the overriding claims of racing, cricket, astronauts or the Chancellor of the Exchequer, but because I am concerned with our assessment of priorities . . .

One of the difficulties of planning programmes for children is the shortage of audience research. For example, we do not have detailed information about children's reactions to programmes comparable to that available about adults' reactions. But the response we get from children's letters constantly reminds us that it is an audience of individuals we are seeking to satisfy, and I believe, because they are television viewers at their most impressionable and receptive period of their lives, that we ought to give their programmes even more careful consideration than those of adults.

At that stage, the output of BBC Television's Children's Department was between nine and ten and a half hours a week including *Play School* repeats, and about one and a half or two hours a week were made for children by drama and light entertainment. (See the table on pages 40–1.) ITV was scheduling six and three-quarter hours of children's programmes.

In the same report, Monica Sims made a point about American cartoons and their popularity.

American cartoons whether comedy like *Deputy Dawg* and *Tom and Jerry* or adventures like *Journey to the Centre of the Earth* or *Marine Boy* always attract a very high proportion of satisfied child viewers, even though their parents may sometimes object to the use of American material or to the fact that the programmes are not informative or uplifting. My own view is that such comedy cartoons are first-class entertainment and are so expensive to make that we could never afford to make our own.

She also said that good, expensive material was bought from Europe and dubbed – unusually for British television which, on the whole, resists the use of dubbing in adult programmes. But she also made the point that the department itself was unable to make programmes of the quality of the French live-action drama *Belle and Sebastian* and emphasized that BBC children's programmes were facing strong competition from the commercial companies. This was the time when *Magpie* was created by Thames Television to compete with *Blue Peter*. There were also a number of innovative entertainment programmes like Associated Rediffusion's *Do Not Adjust Your Set*.

She ended her report by quoting a letter from a child to *The Magic Roundabout*:

Dear Doogool,
I hope u lic the sujar lump, luv Rupert

Output of Children's Department (1969)

BBC1	Monday	Tuesday	Wednesday	Thursday	Friday
4.20 p.m.		*Play School*	*Play School*	*Play School*	*Play School*
4.40 p.m.	*Jackanory*	*Jackanory*	*Jackanory*	*Jackanory*	*Jackanory*
4.55 p.m.	*Blue Peter*	American series: either adventure, cartoon or live action (e.g. *Casey Jones)	Comedy cartoon	*Blue Peter*	*Crackerjack or *Basil Brush (Light Entertainment)
5.20 p.m.	Dubbed film drama serial (e.g. *The Flashing Blade) or English serial (e.g. Adventure Weekly)	*Tom Tom* (or *Vision On*)	*Animal Magic* (or *Wild World*)	European films	*Junior Points of View*

5.45 p.m. *The Magic Roundabout* or other puppet bedtime story

Saturday morning (winter)	12.05–12.25 p.m.	*Laurel and Hardy* or cartoon
	12.25–12.40 p.m.	*Zokko*
Saturday afternoon	5.15 p.m.	**Dr Who* (Drama Department)
Sunday	5.30 p.m.	**Classic serial (Drama Department)
	5.55–6.05 p.m.	*Tom and Jerry* or puppet series (e.g. *Ken Dodd and the Diddymen*)
BBC 2	**Monday-Friday**	
11 a.m.	*Play School*	

* Not made by the Children's Department, but watched by children.

The output of the Children's Department in 1969 is shown in the table above. When Monica Sims left in 1978, it had expanded and changed considerably. She was determined to restore the Children's Department to its former stature, and indeed to expand it. It was she who re-established a proper children's drama output, nurtured *Grange Hill*, developed Saturday morning programming and supported the creation of *John Craven's Newsround*. Other major ingredients at this time were the series bought in by Peggy Miller, the best remembered of which are *The Singing Ringing Tree*, *The White Horses* and *Robinson Crusoe*. It was also during these years that children's programming expanded into Saturday afternoon transmissions with *Play Away* and early evening programming on BBC 2.

By the late 1970s, the output of the Children's Department was varied and rich. The 1978/79 season included factual programmes (*Record Breakers*, *Think of a Number*, *The Story Beneath the Sands*, *John Craven's Newsround*); sport (*We Are the Champions*); drama (*Grange Hill*, *The Moon Stallion*); comedy (*Graham's Gang*); the arts (*Take Hart*); entertainment (*Screen Test*, a film quiz); and *Blue Peter*, *Play School* and *Multi-Coloured Swap Shop*.

Monica Sims was, and still is, a great fighter for children's programmes. She believed passionately that the child audience deserved the best possible service and she, like her predecessors, fought hard to increase the range of programming and the BBC's investment in it.

She was understandably concerned in 1972 when the only mention of children's television programmes during the BBC's fiftieth birthday celebrations concerned *Muffin the Mule*.

Head of Children's Programmes, Television (Monica Sims) to Controller of Programmes, Television (Huw Wheldon), 14 November 1972:

Every other department in television has been credited with some development in twenty-five years except for children's programmes which appear to remain frozen in the early images of their first tentative steps. I am not only thinking of our present output but the considerable achievements when Freda Lingstrom and Owen Reed were laying the foundations for what people still consider a unique television service for children.

This memo was written at the time when the great *Sesame Street* argument was in full flow. *Sesame Street* was a product of the Children's Television Workshop in New York and the brainchild of Joan Ganz Cooney. American children's televison was notoriously bad, and the Children's Television Workshop was set up to create high-quality programming for the public broadcasting system. *Sesame Street* was originally intended as a programme primarily for deprived, inner-city, pre-school children. Its aim was to teach language, number and social skills, and its techniques were revolutionary. It used the quick-cutting, attention-grabbing style of commercials and used advertising techniques to help children learn letters and numbers.

A great deal of money and talent was invested in the show. Jim Henson created the puppet characters – the first Muppets – and the programmes were full of colour and humour. They were totally different in style and pace to the BBC's *Play School* or ITV's *Romper Room*, which was based on a Canadian format, or *Rainbow*. Moreover, the culture and language was overwhelmingly American; in those days, the English language was much less Americanized than it is today.

Sesame Street was offered to the BBC who turned it down. There were a number of reasons. Firstly, the BBC had its own pre-school programme in *Play School*, which catered specifically to its own audience, and it was felt that there was no need for another. Secondly, there was a strong feeling that there were educational dangers in the constant use of repetition and fast pace. Thirdly, it was felt that children would be confused by the language: 'trash can', for instance, for dustbin. Finally, if the programme had been bought

Snuffy and Big Bird from *Sesame Street*, produced by the United States Children's Television Workshop. (Channel 4)

complete, *Play School* and *Watch with Mother* would have been cancelled due to lack of money.

The BBC would have been prepared, and indeed wanted, to buy segments, but the Children's Television Workshop would not agree to this. (It is worth noting that later, when the programme was sold in other foreign markets, this is exactly what did happen.)

Monica Sims was heavily criticized for not buying the programme, and the American press accused her of 'banning' *Sesame Street*. It must have been one of the few occasions when children's programmes made international headlines.

Her views are contained in an article which she wrote for the *New York Times*:

A few weeks ago I was surprised at the reaction to my reference to *Sesame Street* at a press conference in London, announcing the BBC's winter schedule of children's programmes. It was interpreted as a sudden and dramatic ban, but was of course nothing of the kind. It was a decision not to purchase, and had been made public for many months. Let me explain our reasons, and first let me make it absolutely clear that I greatly admire the tremendous achievement of the Children's Television Workshop, particularly in focusing attention on television for younger children in the United States, for taking the needs of young children seriously and for creating an expensive high-quality entertainment programme without constant interruptions for commercials. I am a devoted fan of the Muppets and many of the animated film sequences, and I enjoy the specially composed music and the programme's humour. Last year I was a member of the jury of the *Prix Jeunesse* in Munich which awarded *Sesame Street* a major international prize, and whatever some press reports may have suggested, the doubts I have about the suitability of the programme in our own BBC schedule are not the result of chauvinism or arrogance.

One of our objections to *Sesame Street* as a daily pre-school programme in Britain is that it seems to us more suitable for five- and six-year-olds than for the two-, three- and four-year-olds who comprise our own daytime out-of-school audience.

Our education advisers say that an hour is too long to encourage children under five to keep still and watch television, and we prefer a variety of shorter programmes for them to watch with total concentration to an acceptance of wandering in and out. We also feel that for this very young age, learning letters and numbers is not necessarily the one vital key to success in school or in life. I personally believe that learning by repetition can be useful and enjoyable, and it certainly provides one of the most entertaining elements of *Sesame Street*, but I think that it is even more important to arouse in three- and four-year-old children the desire to learn and find out, wonder, think, imagine, build, watch, listen, feel and help, and to experiment with water, textures, shapes, colours, movements and sounds.

I am reported as saying that I regard *Sesame Street* as 'non democratic'. This is not a word I have ever used. I did use the word authoritarian in the sense that any use of commercial techniques is by implication authoritarian. A commercial's intention is to sell something, to persuade one product is the best. The use of advertising methods in *Sesame Street* to help children recognize and remember letters and numbers is undoubtedly entertaining and legitimate, but we ourselves choose a different approach.

In all our programmes we try to help children to think for themselves and understand the reasons behind any statement. In our own programmes for this age-group we don't say 'this is right or wrong' and 'how clever you are to get it right', but rather 'can you help me sort this out, what are your ideas'. We do not seek to pose questions that have right or wrong answers but rather to encourage the child to put his own questions arising out of his own experience, and we try to extend this experience by showing him more of real life.

Sesame Street was eventually bought and transmitted by London Weekend Television and it still runs in the Channel 4 schedules. There is no doubt that it has had an impact on children's television world-wide. It is now shown in seventy-eight countries. The Muppets became world famous and the whole style and pace of children's programmes was affected. However, *Sesame Street* also raises the whole question of cultural imperialism. How far should television programmes, especially for children, reflect national or international culture? Buying and selling television programmes is big business, and organizations like CTW, Disney and, equally, the BBC have power in the market-place. In 1992, the Australian Children's Film and Television Foundation was planning a new and ambitious early learning programme. It will be interesting to see if it raises the kind of argument *Sesame Street* raised in its time.

During the 1960s and 1970s ITV's children's programmes fluctuated. There were several attempts to put together a strong and competitive children's schedule. However, it was more difficult for children's producers within the individual companies to gain recognition. Also, because each ITV company is a separate and competitive entity, it was hard to put together a coherent schedule, a problem exacerbated by the relationship between the major and the regional companies. In 1973, at an IBA consultation with the ITV companies, Francis Essex made a plea for those concerned with children's programming to formulate, and work together to create, an overall policy overriding individual company ambitions. He wanted to create one pro- gramme daily, on the air from 4.20 p.m. until 6 p.m., introduced by a permanent host and a signature tune. This policy was finally put into operation after the next IBA consultation, in 1981.

Co-ordination during the 1960s and 1970s was carried out by the Children's Sub-Committee which varied in terms of its power and effec- tiveness. In 1968, it was briefly chaired by Doreen Stephens who, together with Joy Whitby the original producer of *Play School* and *Jackanory*, had left the BBC for London Weekend Television. From 1967 Joy Whitby headed a children's department at LWT which made a new magazine programme, called *Tickertape*, and some drama. But the department did not survive for long and programmes aimed at children were devolved to mainstream production departments. Thames, headed by Lewis Rudd from 1970 to 1972 and by Sue Turner from 1972 to 1978, was a major provider of children's programmes

Magpie: Susan Stranks joined by new presenters Douglas Rae and Mick Robertson (behind). (Thames TV, 1972)

during this time. They included *Magpie*, ITV's answer to *Blue Peter*, *Rainbow*, the long-running, pre-school series (1972–), and some dramas, among them *The Warrior Queen* (1978) and *The Tomorrow People* (1973–79; 1992).

Associated Television was well established in the 1960s with Jean Morton's popular *The Tingha and Tucker Club* in 1962 and with Gerry Anderson's cult puppet series *Thunderbirds* in 1965.

Southern Television was the main regional provider of children's programmes to the ITV network, led first by Jack Hargreaves and then by Lewis Rudd. Lewis Rudd remembers that when he came into children's programmes at the end of 1966 ITV was just emerging from a period of very dull scheduling when the main programmes ran for fifty-two weeks a year. Associated Rediffusion made a twice-weekly magazine called *Five O'Clock Club*, ATV a programme called *Junior Sportsweek*, and Granada made *Junior Criss-Cross Quiz* and *Zoo Time*. The last was an outside broadcast from London Zoo fronted by Desmond Morris. The jewel in Rediffusion's crown was probably the drama series *Orlando*, a spin-off from an adult series called *Crane*. It was a heavy production at fifty-two episodes a year, with a tight schedule. Exterior filming was on Monday, and rehearsals were on Tuesday, Wednesday and Thursday. The studio was set on Friday morning, the recording was done in the afternoon and they started all over again the following Monday.

Five O'Clock Club was replaced by a twice-weekly programme, *Disney Wonderland*, whose first presenter was Francesca Annis. The ubiquitous Tony Hart was in the studio drawing Disney characters. The studio items involved Disney character costumes which had been designed for public appearances and therefore had no mouth animation. They were not really meant to be seen in television close-ups. Peter Hawkins sat at a table in the studio doing the voices

Jack Hargreaves fronted a programme called *Country Boy*, the idea of which was to show the countryside to city children. Hargreaves strongly believed in showing the reality of country life. At the 1973 IBA consultation he made a point about the need to tell children the truth and to consider the morality of the choice of subject matter. He described how, at a *Prix Jeunesse* discussion he had been violently attacked by other delegates because of an episode in *Country Boy* where squirrels were shot by gamekeepers because they were destroying young trees. Scandinavians, in particular, thought this was a shocking thing to show children. Later, the Finnish delegation showed a cartoon about a lynx which promised to be good and not eat birds any more. This programme subsequently won a prize. Hargreaves had pointed out to the producer that it was a lie to suggest that a lynx was good if it promised not to eat birds, since all that would happen was that it would die of starvation! It was the duty of children's programme-makers to be honest.

Southern produced the long-running *How* which ended in 1981 when the company lost its franchise, only to be revived in 1990 as *How 2*. *Runaround* was another production from Southern, who also supplied a considerable amount of drama including *The Flockton Flyer*, *The Famous Five* and *Worzel Gummidge*. ITV also entered the Saturday morning arena, most notably with *Tiswas* from ATV. This was networked from 1975 and aroused much controversy because of its anarchic style.

By the end of the 1970s both the BBC and ITV were providing a considerable variety of programmes for children. In the early 1980s, the general pattern remained much the same, give or take cut-backs and periods of expansion or fluctuation caused by the change of the ITV franchises. However, towards the end of the 1980s, with the new age of multi-channel, lightly regulated broadcasting in sight, the scenario started to change once more.

CHAPTER TWO

Puppets and Pre-school Programmes

Programmes for small children often seem to be the best remembered and the most loved. The astonishing success of the BBC's *Watch with Mother* video (over half a million sales between 1986 and early 1992) shows this, as did the outcry when the programme disappeared in 1980 and when *Play School* was replaced by *Playdays* in 1988. These were some of the *Play School* headlines and stories:

Please Don't Dump Humpty (*Daily Mirror*)

A Great Fall, Victoria Coren Weeps For Play School (*Daily Telegraph*)

Last Turn Of The Lock
What Michael Grade has done to Ms Mavis Nicholson, Miss Home plans to do to Jemima and Co. They will not have their contracts renewed in the new updated format. Like Bill and Ben (and, of course, Little Weed), Andy Pandy, and the Woodentops before them – and, long ago, for those who remember, such unseen stalwarts as Larry the Lamb, Mr Growser, and Norman and Henry Bones (the boy detectives) – they are doomed to survive from now on only as cherished memories among those whom they saw through childhood. (*Guardian*)

Humpty Dumpty Dumped, Beeb Faces Backlash On Play School Chop
Wicked Auntie Beeb is set to axe four of TV's top stars. Big Ted, Little Ted, Jemima and Humpty are to be banished from the screens . . . to a glass case in a museum. For after 25 years, the popular toddlers' show *Play School* is getting the boot. BBC bosses say the programme is 'out of date'. But the move is certain to infuriate millions of mums and dads who have trusted *Play School* not to scare, indoctrinate or confuse their children. (*Daily Star*)

In the 1950s, puppets played an important role. Muffin the Mule, together with Annette Mills, was among the first real television stars soon to be followed by Andy Pandy, Sooty and Bill and Ben. Adults today still remember the magic of the jingle which introduced the early programmes:

> Here comes Muffin, Muffin the mule,
> Dear old Muffin, playing the fool.
> Here comes Muffin, everybody sing,
> Here comes Muffin the mule.

Muffin the Mule, the first star of children's television, with Annette Mills. (BBC, 1952)

Andy Pandy with his friends Looby Loo and Teddy. (BBC, 1952)

Freda Lingstrom and Maria Bird were the creative force behind Andy Pandy and Bill and Ben who soon followed Muffin in television popularity. Both Audrey Atterbury, 'who pulls the strings', and Peter Hawkins, who provided the voices, remember rehearsing on Freda's garden wall in Westerham because it was the right height for the puppets. From 1955 to 1958 rehearsals and filming took place in a tin shed in the Lime Grove Studio complex and in 1960 the team moved to a purpose-built puppet studio in TV Centre.

In those days the programmes were made in very long takes which was exhausting for operators and actors. There was hardly any opportunity to edit and it is not surprising that these early programmes now look a little basic. However, there is no doubt that characters made their mark and remained newsworthy. Bill and Ben and the Woodentops made headline news when they were stolen on their way to a children's exhibition in Edinburgh, and when they reappeared in a London auction room. During the 1970s the

The Flowerpot Men, better known as Bill and Ben. (BBC, 1952)

black-and-white prints of Andy Pandy became too poor to use and they were remade in colour, in the Abbey Road Studios of Beatles fame.

Some of the early puppet programmes were ambitious. Gordon Murray, who worked in the BBC Children's Department in the early 1950s, created a fantasy series called *Rubovia*. It consisted of original plays performed by the BBC Puppet Theatre and they had titles like *Clocks and Blocks*, *Zara Knows All* and *Knight for a Day*. Derek Nimmo frequently appeared in the cast as one of the voices. Gordon Murray's team also adapted a number of well-known stories for puppet plays, including Hans Christian Andersen's *The Emperor's Nightingale* (1958) and John Ruskin's *The King of the Golden River*

The King and the Chamberlain in another Rubovian legend – *Something in the Air* – created by Gordon Murray. (BBC, 1960)

Producer Gordon Murray directing his puppeteers on *The Emperor's New Clothes*. (BBC, 1958)

(1959). Most of the early puppets were string puppets but it was not long before glove puppets began to make their mark.

Sooty is one of the most famous and long-lived of these. Like many others, the bear's rise to fame was really pure chance. In 1948 Harry Corbett took his family on holiday to Blackpool where he bought the puppet to amuse his children. But Sooty was soon incorporated into the amateur magic act which Harry did at children's parties and other functions. In 1952 he managed to get an audition with the BBC in Manchester and he and Sooty made their first television appearance on a show called *Talent Night*, compered by Jimmy James and introduced by McDonald Hobley. It was a success. The *Sunday*

Express of 4 May 1952 said: 'Five minutes on the television screen last night established Harry Corbett's teddy bear as a rival to Muffin the Mule.'

Freda Lingstrom believed that Sooty would be a great success and he became part of a new series called *Saturday Special*. His career was launched. By 1955, he had his own show: *The Sooty Show*. Sweep the dog joined the team in 1957 and Soo, a panda girlfriend for Sooty, was introduced in 1964 – but not without much heart-searching by the BBC who were concerned that sex might be creeping into the show.

Harry Corbett and Sooty remained a successful part of the BBC children's schedule until 1967 when a number of long-established shows were axed. Harry Corbett blamed the incoming Controller of BBC 1, Paul Fox, but it is more likely that the axing was on the advice of Ursula Eason, who felt there was a lack of new ideas for the shows. In any case, Sooty made a swift move across to ITV, to Thames Television, where he remained until they lost their franchise in 1992, although now in partnership with Harry Corbett's son Matthew. Granada TV signed up Sooty for a new series in 1993.

Harry Corbett and Sooty. (BBC, 1955)

Matthew Corbett with Sooty, Sweep and Soo. (Thames TV, 1991)

Puppets like Sooty become real characters and as famous as human stars. In recent times Gordon the Gopher, who started as a prop for Phillip Schofield in 1986, and Edd the Duck, who first appeared with Andy Crane in 1988, have risen to fame. They have their own fan mail and huge followings.

The best-known character puppets in the early days of ITV's children's television were probably Tingha and Tucker, two koala bears. Jean Morton was the in-vision continuity announcer for Associated Television in the Midlands. In the early 1960s someone sent her two koala bear toys from Australia as a present and, almost as a joke, she showed them on the screen one evening. They were an instant hit and soon had their own show: *The Tingha and Tucker Club*. Children were invited to join the club and it soon had a membership – they stopped counting after registering 750 000. *Tingha and Tucker* was a five-day-a-week series. In the late 1960s there was a Sunday series *The Tree House Family*, in which Tingha and Tucker and other characters like Willie the Wombat appeared with Jean Morton reading bible stories. There were huge annual meetings of Tingha and Tucker Club members. On one occasion, at Woburn in Bedfordshire, Lew Grade (later Lord Grade), Chairman and Managing Director of ATV, was bemused to see thousands of children rushing around apparently with their fingers up their noses. They were in fact giving the Tingha and Tucker Club secret sign: 'index finger on bridge of nose'.

Jean Morton with Tingha and Tucker. (ATV, 1963)

Basil Brush gets his own series and a new partner – 'Mr Rodney' Bewes. (BBC, 1968)

Over the years there have been many character puppets, but perhaps one of the best loved is Basil Brush with his 'boom boom' catch-phrase, provided by Ivan Owen, and his luckless side-kicks who included Mr Rodney (Rodney Bewes) and Mr Derek (Derek Fowlds). All these puppets were traditional in style and adapted to television.

The first real television puppets were probably Jim Henson's Muppets. They made their first appearance in *Sesame Street* in 1969, and in their own show in 1976. Kermit was basically a very simple concept: a sock with a hand inside it. Jim Henson firmly believed that the television puppeteer had to learn the grammar of television and be prepared to use and exploit the medium's technology. He pursued this theory and developed extraordinary techniques which he used in *Fraggle Rock* with electronically controlled puppets, and later in feature films and the television series *The Storyteller* where he created complex creatures operated by puppeteers and technicians.

The Muppet Show was aimed as much at adults as it was at children, but there is no doubt that all the Henson characters like Big Bird, Miss Piggy, and Kermit have huge child appeal. Jim Henson, who died in 1990, was an innovator and a carer, someone who will be much missed in the world of children's entertainment. Few people who were there will forget the amazing

Jim Henson, creator of *The Muppets*, with Kermit the Frog. (ATV, 1976)

memorial service in St Paul's, London, the cathedral decorated with silver birch and foxgloves and the puppets singing at the altar rail to a congregation of adults and small children standing on seats to get a better look.

In recent years in Britain there has been another development in puppet-making for television which could be called the 'Spitting Image School'. *Spitting Image* was obviously a satirical programme for adults but it affected the style of puppets for children. The crocodile in ITV's *Round the Bend* and the puppets in the BBC's series *Dizzy Heights* are examples. One puppet who is given credit for saving a whole television station is Roland Rat, created and operated by David Claridge. Ann Wood, who was in charge of children's programmes for ITV's TV-am, discovered him and he came to the aid of the ailing station when editor-in-chief Greg Dyke decided to give him his own morning show to boost ratings in July 1983. Roland Rat became a superstar overnight, reviving TV-am's ratings so efficiently that the station retained its franchise, at that time at least.

Doc Croc and friends from *Round the Bend*. (Yorkshire TV, 1989)

Roland Rat (operated by David Claridge) who saved TV-am and later had his own series on BBC TV.

In 1991, the BBC purchased *Thunderbirds*, the Gerry Anderson adventure series originally broadcast by ITV in 1965. Gerry Anderson started as a film technician and dubbing editor. His first venture into puppetry was *The Adventures of Twizzle* in 1957 with Roberta Leigh for Associated Rediffusion. This used very basic papier mâché puppets against a painted backing. Anderson was ashamed of the outcome and decided his role in life was to make 'really terrific puppet films'. His first major series was *Four Feather Falls* in 1960 for Granada, followed in 1961 by *Supercar* for ATV. Lew Grade became his patron and Gerry Anderson went on to huge success both in Britain and America with *Fireball XL5* (1962), *Stingray* (1964) and *Thunderbirds*.

Thunderbirds is probably the best-remembered series, telling of the exploits of International Rescue led by Jeff Tracey and his four sons. There was also the glamorous Lady Penelope, who travelled by Rolls-Royce, and her chauffeur, Parker, who was based on a waiter in the King's Arms at Cookham who had once worked at Windsor Castle. As with Jim Henson, Gerry Anderson's puppets grew more and more complex over the years. However,

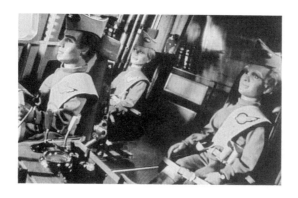

Thunderbirds take to the air again. (ATV 1965/ BBC 1991)

Thunderbirds is still best remembered for its only too visible 'invisible' strings. The ratings for *Thunderbirds* on BBC 2 in 1991 show that there is still an audience for the series. In fact, the manufacturers of toys based on the puppets was caught out that Christmas time: they had not foreseen the likely impact that the series would have on a new generation and there were not enough toys in the shops.

Puppets also appear in animated series, using a technique called stop-frame. In this, the puppets are placed in sets and their articulated bodies are moved by the animators and filmed shot by shot. Nowadays these techniques are highly sophisticated, but in the early days people developed ideas as they went along. Oliver Postgate and Peter Firmin were among the pioneers who, in the late 1950s, worked with Associated Rediffusion in both stop-frame and drawn animation techniques. They worked in a so-called studio full of junk and cast-off Meccano sets and created their own equipment. *Pogles' Wood*, transmitted by the BBC from 1966 to 1967 in the *Watch with Mother* series, is one of their creations and among their best remembered. The pink knitted Clangers (1969) who communicated in whistles and the lugubrious Bagpuss (1974) were also theirs.

Another pair who started in a similar small-scale domestic way, but have now expanded into a much bigger business, are Brian Cosgrove and Mark Hall. They both worked as graphic artists in ITV and came together in 1971 to form Cosgrove Hall in a converted warehouse in the Manchester suburb of Chorlton cum Hardy. Cosgrove Hall have developed model animation to a fine art: *The Pied Piper of Hamlyn* (1981) and *The Wind in the Willows* (1984–88) are examples of programmes they have done for ITV. They also

Peter Firmin and Oliver Postgate, creators of *Pogles' Wood*, with Mr Pogle and Pippin. (BBC, 1966)

Bagpuss watches over his creator Peter Firmin. (BBC, 1974)

The Wombles of Wimbledon Common. (BBC, 1973)

work in cell animation, the traditional Disney kind of animation. Among their most successful series in this genre have been *Dangermouse* (1981) and *Count Duckula* (1988). The latter, about a vegetarian vampire duck, was made as a co-production with the American cable company Nickelodeon.

Cosgrove Hall is a subsidiary of Thames Television. Central Television also had an animation arm, Filmfair, which was founded by the late Graham Clutterbuck. It played an important role in providing series for children's television. The company was sold to The Storm Group in 1991. *Paddington*, based on the Michael Bond stories and made in very basic animation, was one of its most important productions. The original series, first broadcast in 1976 with the incomparable voice of Michael Hordern, is likely to be remembered long after its updated, technically superior, mid-Atlantic, 1990s successor is forgotten. Another well-remembered favourite is *The Wombles* based on Elisabeth Beresford's ecology-minded creatures from Wimbledon Common.

Above: The firemen come to the rescue in *Trumpton*; created by Gordon Murray. (BBC, 1967)

Below: (from left to right) *Rainbow* presenter Geoffrey Hayes with singers Roger Walker, Jane Tucker and Rod Burton, and puppets Zippy, George and Bungle. (Thames TV, 1978)

Above: Postman Pat with Ted Glen; created by Ivor Wood. (BBC, 1981)

Below: Mole and Ratty from *The Wind in the Willows*; produced by Cosgrove Hall. (Thames TV, 1984)

Above: The Town Mouse and the Country Mouse; illustrated by Mina Martinez for *Play School*. (BBC, 1971)

Below: The Why Bird from *Playdays*; created by Felgate Productions. (BBC, 1988)

Above left: Una Stubbs as Aunt Sally with Jon Pertwee, star of *Worzel Gummidge*. (Southern TV, 1979) *Above right: The Secret Garden* featuring Sarah Hollis Andrews as Mary Lennox. (BBC, 1975) *Below:* Todd Carty as Tucker Jenkins (far left) with his school friends from *Grange Hill*. (BBC, 1981)

Above left: Tony Robinson telling his story *Skulduggery* for the Silver Jubilee season of *Jackanory*. (BBC 1991) *Above right:* Kenneth Williams reading Roald Dahl's *James and the Giant Peach* on *Jackanory*. (BBC, 1986) *Below:* Bernard Cribbins reading Kenneth Grahame's *The Wind in the Willows* on *Jackanory*. (BBC, 1982)

Above: The Chronicles of Narnia: David Thwaites as Eustace, Tom Baker as Puddleglum, and Camilla Power as Jill. (BBC, 1990) *Below left:* Devin Stanfield as Kay Harker looking into the Box of Delights. (BBC, 1984) *Below right:* Richard O'Brien in *The Crystal Maze*; made by Chatsworth Productions. (Channel 4, 1990)

Above: Roy Castle and Norris McWhirter with the world's largest penknife in *Record Breakers*. (BBC, 1978)
Below: Phillip Schofield interviewing Jason Donovan in the *Going Live!* studio. (BBC, 1991)

Above left: Gordon the Gopher from *Going Live!* (BBC, 1987)
Above right: Edd the Duck wearing his *Blue Peter* jumper. (BBC)

Below: Pingu, created by Otmar Gutmann of Trickfilmstudio in Germany. (BBC, 1991)

The BBC has commissioned its animation from a number of different companies over the years, but for a time it had its own embryonic animation unit headed by Hilary Hayton. It was a spin-off from a special graphics department created for *Play School*. The unit did a series of stories based on distinguished picture-books by people like writer and illustrator Michael Foreman and Brian Wildsmith, artist and maker of picture-books for children. The operation was very small scale, with one animator and one paint-and-trace person working on the cell animation. *Crystal Tipps and Alistair* started within this unit but went outside in 1972 when it expanded to a series of twenty-five five-minute programmes. The unit never developed and the BBC continued in its tradition of commissioning from outside companies.

One of the people who worked with Graham Clutterbuck and later set up on his own was Ivor Wood, who had originally worked in Paris with Serge Danot on *The Magic Roundabout*. Ivor Wood's best-known series, *Postman Pat*, first transmitted in 1981 by the BBC, became something of a phenomenon. It started in Ivor Wood's garage in South Kensington in London, but was firmly based in the reality of the Lake District and even on a real postman.

Nearly all animated series have spin-offs in terms of books, records and other merchandising. Sooty was very aggressively merchandised in the 1950s and became a big business. Most series do reasonably well in terms of making money but some are extraordinary successes. *Postman Pat* was one of these. One of the reasons was that Terry Wogan took it up on his Radio 2 breakfast show. He originally played a record of the programme's signature tune as a joke, and from then on it snowballed. Postman Pat is now a household word and beloved by the Post Office as a public relations symbol.

Many puppet animation series had traditional, often rural, settings: the BBC's *Postman Pat*, *Camberwick Green*, *Trumpton* and *Fireman Sam* and ITV's *Thomas the Tank Engine*. (The last is one of few British animation series which has made a successful transition to American network television.) However, to balance this, the BBC commissioned *Bertha* (1985) which is set in a factory and has multi-ethnic characters and, more recently, *Joshua Jones* (1992) which is set on a canal that passes through both urban and rural settings.

Until 1984, the BBC ended its transmission for children with a five-minute slot immediately before the early evening news. It was here that *The Magic Roundabout* was played and became another television legend. The series, created by Serge Danot in the early 1960s for French television, started life in humble surroundings in one room in a derelict house in Paris. The fuses kept blowing because of the amount of electricity used by the lights on the sets. The series was discovered in Europe by Doreen Stephens, who asked Joy Whitby, then in charge of *Play School*, to suggest someone to do the voices. She suggested Eric Thompson, an actor who was currently one of the *Play School* presenters. He did not work from translations of the French scripts but made up stories to fit the pictures. *The Magic Roundabout*, first broadcast in 1965, soon became a favourite with both adults and children and achieved high ratings. A new series, voiced by Nigel Planer, was shown on Channel 4 in 1992.

Animation series seem to create cult followings and generate strange stories. There were rumours that *The Magic Roundabout* was a coded

The Magic Roundabout surrounded by Dougal and friends. (BBC, 1966)

message about drug culture and, earlier, that the jolly *Captain Pugwash* series, first broadcast in 1957, contained deliberate sexual puns and innuendoes. Neither story has any foundation.

For many years the BBC and the large ITV companies were the main commissioners of children's animation but the Welsh channel, S4C, which began broadcasting in 1982, has become a major player, co-producing with other companies and generating a real if small-scale animation industry in Wales and the West of England.

Its most recent venture for children is a series of Shakespeare plays adapted into half-hour scripts by the distinguished children's writer Leon Garfield. The animation is by six different Russian animation directors from Soyuzmutifilm. Each play is in a different style of animation and the voices are those of leading Shakespearian actors like Timothy West, Daniel Massey and Zoe Wannamaker. This project, together with other exciting developments, has been masterminded by Chris Grace, Controller of Animation for S4C, who has done a great deal to widen the scope of animation in Britain.

Both the BBC and ITV buy animation from overseas, mainly from North America. Series such as *Thundercats, He Man* and *Teenage Mutant Hero (Ninja) Turtles* are usually aimed at older children, but some cater for the younger age-group. *Babar the Elephant* and *Ewoks* are examples. These older series are often criticized for being too violent, too North American, too mindless or too commercial. There are two main reasons why they are bought. Firstly, they are very popular and support more difficult material in the schedule. Secondly, they are relatively cheap.

Animation of all kinds is very expensive to make, ranging from £4000 to £25 000 per minute. It is impossible to fund enough United Kingdom animation and that is why Anglo-American and Anglo-European co-production deals are becoming more and more frequent. The BBC has worked with Hanna Barbera in the United States and is currently working with France Animation; TVS co-produced *Rupert* with Nelvana in Canada in 1991. There is no equivalent in Britain of Disney or Hanna Barbera and, unless there is a major investment, animation in the United Kingdom seems likely to remain a relatively small-scale operation. Perhaps that is no bad thing when one looks at the inferior quality of some of the series of 165 half-hours that come pouring out of North America but are largely made in Korea, Taiwan and Japan. There is big money to be made from international distribution and merchandising, particularly of classic stories, out of copyright, which are used for animation series. Animation is easy to dub – there are no problems with matching actors' voices to film footage. And when it is relatively low quality and produced in volume the costs can be amortized. The overall standard of animation in the world market is not, with some honourable exceptions, particularly high and, as there is always more air-time to fill, there seems little prospect of it improving.

There are attempts to get Europe working more coherently in the world of animation. Cartoon Forum is a European Economic Community initiative which brings animators and buyers together and encourages co-operation between groups of animators. European animation companies tend to be small and fairly isolated, so co-operation is useful to achieve greater volume and speed of production. The opening up of Eastern Europe will certainly have an effect on the world animation scene. Another project of interest is the European Broadcasting Union co-production of *The Animals of Farthing Wood*, due for transmission in Europe in January 1993. Based on the books by Colin Dann, this is a twenty-six-part series, funded by nineteen countries and made half in the United Kingdom by Telemagination and half in France by La Fabrique. The aim is to create a series which is specifically European in style and feel. If it is a success, other projects may be put together in the same way. It may well be that, in years to come, there will be a recognizable European animation style to challenge that of North America.

When BBC 2 started in 1964 it introduced a new kind of programme for pre-school children. Michael Peacock, Chief of Programmes for the new channel, invited Joy Whitby, formerly a producer of radio's *Listen with Mother*, to create a new daily programme for young children which would be innovative and challenging. She was given a blank sheet of paper and *Play School* was created in the aftermath of the upheaval when the Children's Department was merged with Women's Programmes to form Family Programmes. Doreen Stephens, head of the new department, became a strong supporter of the programme. *Play School* was appropriate for its time as it was created when there was great deal of debate about the poor provision of nursery education.

Joy Whitby brought in a number of advisers, notably Nancy Quayle, an ex-nursery-school teacher, who had very strong views on what was and was not right for the under-five age-group. Mary Waddington was an expert in early learning and Judy Taylor from the Bodley Head, where she was then children's editor and later deputy managing director, advised on fiction. Joy Whitby wanted a programme that would be less arch and middle class than *Watch with Mother*, with presenters who were young, natural and friendly. However, she also believed that children should experience people of all ages. It was significant that the first *Play School* story-teller was the septuagenarian Athene Seyler who told the traditional tale *Little Red Hen*.

The *Play School* team was relatively inexperienced in television terms. Cynthia Felgate, production assistant, had experience in children's theatre

and a little television. Molly Cox and I came from radio as production assistant and research assistant respectively. Daphne Jones, also a research assistant, had been a producer's assistant in Women's Programmes. We all wrote and directed as part of our duties. There were others who were refugees from the 'break-up'. Dorothea Brooking, for instance, had huge experience – she was one of the original children's producers in 1950 – and was able to help the newcomers. The very first time I ever went on a film location was to Beaconscot model village in Buckinghamshire, with Dorothea Brooking. I was absolutely terrified because to me she was a legend and I knew absolutely nothing about television. However, nobody could have been kinder and more encouraging and I learnt a great deal even on that first day.

The whole team learnt as it went along and the programme evolved as we learnt. There were landmarks from the very beginning: the opening titles, showing a house being formed, and its accompanying jingle:

> Here is a house,
> Here is a door,
> Windows one, two, three, four,
> Ready to knock, turn the lock,
> It's *Play School*.

All these elements changed in design over the years but they remained part of the structure, as did the style of presentation with a different man and woman each week, sometimes joined by other guests.

In the early programmes, items were introduced in rhyme: 'Here are our windows which open wide/To show both town and countryside.' However, the rhymes soon disappeared. Humpty, Jemima, Big Ted and Little Ted were all part of the original set-up, and stayed. Other toys like Hamble, 'the one who sits up and does what she's told', and Dapple, the rocking horse, appeared later.

Play School was the programme that opened BBC 2 at 11 a.m. on 21 April 1964. This was not planned. The grand opening of the channel should have been on the previous night but there was a massive power failure and BBC 2 did not start until the following day. The first image of the new channel was the soon-to-be-familiar house and jingle.

The series ran until 1988, a total of over 5000 programmes. From 1967 until 1987 it was run by Cynthia Felgate, who took over from Joy Whitby. *Play School* was very important within the BBC Children's Department as a place where new production talent was nurtured and trained. Many men and women who worked on the series in the early days of their careers moved on to create, and work on, new programmes and series of their own. Notably Ann Reay, producer of *Play Away*; Peter Ridsdale-Scott, producer of *Cabbages and Kings*; Albert Barber, whose productions include *Think of a Number* and *Grange Hill*; Peter Charlton, producer of *We Are the Champions* and scriptwriter and producer for *Ring-a-Ding*; Michael Cole, who produced *Chock-a-Block* and *Bric-a-Brac* among other programmes and who wrote and produced *Ragtime*; and Anne Gobey, producer and director of *Play Away* and series producer of *Corners*.

The people who worked on *Play School* certainly had to use their initiative. One of the phrases that became a byword was, 'Go and do something imaginative with umbrellas.' The point was that even if it was raining you could probably make quite an interesting film. Because the budgets were small and time was short, nothing was ever wasted. It was an extremely good way of teaching people the value of television resources and what could be done with them.

Play School was very different in style from the programmes that had preceded it. The presenters came mainly from the theatre and often had comedy talent; Gordon Rollings and Brian Cant are examples. The women were chosen to be real people, not cyphers. Names that are well remembered are Julie Stevens, Chloe Ashcroft and Carol Chell. One of the basic philosophies of the programme was to address the individual child at home, not the audience *en masse*, and it was important to encourage participation. Members of the production team used to visit children at home to assess how successful the programme was in this and other areas. Music and songs played an important part; there was always live music in the studio and the musicians became essential members of the team.

The original animals were two budgerigars, two mice called Henry and Henrietta, one rabbit (George) who was later replaced by Peter, and two goldfish. Katoo the cockatoo was a later addition. For most of the life of

Play School (BBC): (top to bottom) Julie Stevens and Terence Holland (Terry Frisby) seeing what's in the useful box. (1964) Rick Jones with Peter the rabbit. (1964) Gordon Rollings and Phyllida Law doing a spot of gardening. (1964) Dressing-up day with Carole Ward and Eric Thompson. (1965) Regular story-teller and guest Ted Moult on his farm in the sixties.

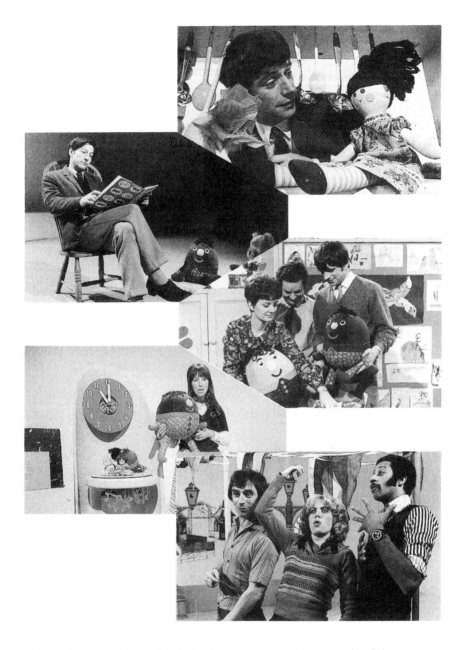

(Top to bottom) Johnny Ball in the kitchen area with Jemima. (1969) The toys listening to Colin Jeavons reading a story in the 1000th edition. (1968) Julie Stevens and Johnny Ball with director Michael Cole packing a Humpty to take to Israel for their version of the programme. (1970) Chloe Ashcroft telling the time on the tenth birthday programme. (1974) Johnny Ball, Carol Leader and Derek Griffiths celebrating the 3000th edition of the programme. (1975)

Play School the pets were looked after by Wendy Duggan, who became the BBC Children's Department animal adviser. On the whole, the animals led very comfortable lives. Goats have travelled regularly in taxis and badgers were known to stop off at cocktail parties. When the show's tadpoles reached froghood, Wendy Duggan would return them to a pond in the middle of Wimbledon Common. There was, however, one unfortunate occasion when a pair of mice that were appearing in the *Play School* pantomime were given too much sedative to calm them down and turned their feet up in the air instead. Viewers were not told that this had happened, but when regular pets died the audience was informed. The team believed that even young children were able to cope with the death of a pet and that it was something that many children needed to share with other people.

Two important elements in *Play School* from the very beginning were 'getting out and about' and encouraging an international outlook. Initially, 'getting out' was mainly on film seen through one of the windows. Some scenes were specially shot and some put together from archive material. In the early days, the 1950s *Children's Newsreels* were a useful source but gradually *Play School* built up a huge film archive of its own. The programme paid regular visits on film to the same place at different seasons – Ted Moult's farm, for example. With the introduction of colour, in 1968, there were occasional outside broadcasts from different locations including Regent's Park Zoo, Bodiam Castle, the about-to-be-opened M40 and later Aviemore and Lyme Regis.

Although *Sesame Street*, first broadcast in the United States in 1969, is often credited with being the first internationally minded pre-school programme, there has been an Australian version of *Play School* from 1966 to the present day, and at various times versions of the programme existed in Italy, Germany, Switzerland, Austria, Norway, Israel, Eire, Canada, Iran, Spain and New Zealand. It was originally sold in kit form and the individual countries adapted scripts, graphics and films as they wished. There was an advantage for the British *Play School* as films were exchanged and children got glimpses of life in other countries.

There were differences between the *Play School*s made in England and those abroad. For example, in Zurich Humpty was nailed down so that he

Romper Room. (Anglia TV, 1964)

would not fall over; the Swiss felt this would be untidy. They also were concerned about Hamble, who was not the neatest of creatures. And they would not use one of the *Play School* classic films made by Daphne Jones about an old lady and her cat because they believed that it reflected a side of life – loneliness in old age – that children should not be aware of. However, *Play School* always believed in being realistic within the terms of its own audience.

To create the *Play School* Graphics Unit, Joy Whitby brought in Hilary Hayton who put together a young and very talented team which included Paul Birkbeck, Graham McCallum and Mina Martinez. They worked on original graphics for *Play School* and, from the mid-1960s, on much of the artwork for *Jackanory*. Their work was innovative and distinctive, giving *Play School* a look that was very much its own. Despite its title and the fact that it was based on sound educational principles, *Play School* never set out to teach in a formal way. In this it differed from its ITV equivalent, *Rainbow*, and, to some extent, its BBC successor *Playdays.*

Rainbow, ITV's long-running pre-school series, started in 1972. There was much debate as to whether or not it should come from the Children's

Department or the Schools Department. In the end, it was decided it should be produced by the Children's Department as this would allow it a bigger budget. However, the programme always had an educational intention and an official education adviser was attached to the production team. Its aim was to develop language and number concepts at a level which would help children to prepare for school.

Rainbow used the same kind of ingredients as *Play School* – songs, stories, films, etc. – but the style of presentation was different. Geoffrey Hayes, the main presenter from 1973, worked with the puppets Bungle, George and Zippy who acted as surrogate children. There was also, at one stage, a singing group, Rod, Jane and Matthew (Corbett) later Rod, Jane and Freddy. The balance between education and entertainment, and the amount of music in the programme, has varied over the years, but *Rainbow*, produced by Charles Warren, has become as much of a household word as *Play School* was in its time. This is despite the fact that it has probably suffered more from pressures in terms of numbers of programmes and scheduling than its BBC equivalent.

The difference in styles between *Rainbow* and *Play School* are interesting. *Play School* relied on direct contact between presenter and child. There were no puppets as such and the toys were used as props not as participants in the action. In *Rainbow*, puppets are used to demonstrate how children might do, or react to, things. In *Play School* there were rarely, if ever, children in the studio. They appeared on film and were generally observed playing on a farm, for example, or flying kites rather than leading the action.

Playdays, originally called *Playbus*, was created by Cynthia Felgate in 1988 to succeed *Play School*. It has much more emphasis on children in active roles. The programme has five different stops, one for each day of the week, and in the 'Playground Stop', for example, children play without adult intervention and, where relevant, make their own comments. There is more emphasis on letters and numbers in *Playdays* than there was in *Play School* but the programme does not attempt formal teaching. In its design and overall style it is an attempt to update pre-school programming to reflect contemporary society (some stories have been partly told in Hindi) while at the same time maintaining the traditional songs and rhymes which are part of

Cynthia Felgate discussing a script with *Play School* presenter Brian Cant. (BBC, mid-60s)

childhood. Puppets, for example the Why Bird and Lizzie, a black marionette, play an important part. If you compare programmes from the early days of *Play School* in 1964 with the early days of *Playdays* you can see how society has changed in the intervening years. Early *Play School* now looks almost twee, although at the time it was considered to be enormously advanced – and, indeed, was so. But it is rooted in an era of toys and nurseries which no longer exists. The much more relaxed, ethnically mixed and colourful *Playdays,* first broadcast in 1988, shows how time has moved on.

Changing well-known formats like *Watch with Mother* and *Play School* causes great concern among viewers. People always tend to feel that change is going to be for the worse. The title *Watch with Mother*, which had been taken from BBC Radio's *Listen with Mother*, was dropped in 1980, although the elements within it were continued in the new *Sea-Saw* strands. The main reason for the change was that large numbers of children at that time were not watching with Mother but were on their own or in groups.

The decision to drop *Play School* was taken after a great deal of thought and debate. When I returned to the BBC from ITV in 1986 I reviewed the whole output in terms of its performance and relevance to the audience. I felt that *Play School* had become stultified in its format and style and, despite a number of attempts to update it in minor ways, a radical change was required. I discussed the issue with pre-school experts including Cynthia Felgate and decided to make the change. Cynthia, who had become an independent producer not long before, tendered for the new project and won the contract. *Playdays* is still developing. In 1992 the 'Dot Stop' was dropped in favour of the 'Roundabout Stop' and other changes will no doubt occur in the future.

Cynthia Felgate, who died in 1991, was one of the most important influences on the development of children's television in this country over the last twenty years. Not only was she responsible for major series like *Play School*, *Playdays* and *Play Away* but she also encouraged smaller-scale series like *Fingermouse* (1985), *Lay on Five* (1985–87), *Corners* (1987–91) and many, many others. Her particular concern was for young children, who she believed could be all too easily exploited by those in search of ratings. As far as Cynthia Felgate was concerned, the very young deserved the very best.

CHAPTER THREE
Story-telling and Drama

Story-telling, a mainstay of BBC Radio's *Children's Hour*, was an important element in the early years of television. Stories were mainly illustrated by puppets or by drawn pictures. *Bengo,* the boxer puppy, was a typical series which was first broadcast in the 1950s and incorporated into *Blue Peter* from 1963 to 1965. Story-telling was also used within programmes like *Studio E* (1957–58) and performers like Vera McKechnie told them.

Johnny Morris, who later became famous as Keeper Morris had a story-telling series called *The Hot Chestnut Man* which started in 1955 as part of

Johnny Morris telling stories as *The Hot Chestnut Man.* (BBC, 1962)

Playbox. He stood with his barrow of hot chestnuts and told a different story each week. The story was an important element in *Play School* and in 1965 Michael Peacock, Chief of Programmes BBC 2, told Joy Whitby there was a spare quarter-hour to fill at tea-time and suggested stories.

Molly Cox and I, who had both been heavily involved in the story-telling element of *Play School*, moved to work on the new programme. It was agreed that it should include all kinds of stories from traditional folk tales to Greek myths and legends and readings from well-known books. The look of the programme was originally very simple and strongly linked to the *Play School* visual style. The story-teller sat on a white, wrought-iron bench. On a matching table beside him or her was an object related to the particular story. In the first week, for the traditional fairy tale *Cap of Rushes*, a jar of bulrushes stood on the table.

The programme started with a kaleidoscope image. Originally this was just a pattern of flowers but later pictures relating to the story dissolved into a close-up of whatever the relevant object was. (The kaleidoscope idea was lifted from a 1950s story-telling programme, *Picture Book*, presented by Patricia Driscoll and later Vera McKechnie.)

Finding a name for the new series was a big problem. The team wanted to avoid the standard 'story book', 'story time' idea, but no one could think of anything better. Time was getting short when Molly Cox and I went away for a holiday in Scotland and, sitting by the fire in a remote cottage, suddenly remembered a nursery rhyme that had something to do with stories. Unfortunately, we could not remember it properly and, as it was a weekend, had a frustrating time until the libraries reopened on Monday morning. This was the line we had half remembered:

> I'll tell you a story of Jackanory
> And now my story's begun,
> I'll tell you another of Jack and his brother
> And now my story's done.

As the Opies' invaluable *Dictionary of English Nursery Rhymes* explained, this was a 'variant' of a political rhyme. The team was quite disappointed when no

Jackanory story-tellers (BBC): (top left) actress Margaret Rutherford (1966), (top right) Master of the Thames sailing barge *The Cambria* Bob Roberts (1966) and (above) illustrator/author Quentin Blake (1976).

one wrote to *The Times* complaining about political bias in the new programme.

Jackanory began in 1965 as a short-term experiment. In 1990, it celebrated its twenty-fifth birthday. During that twenty-five years more than 650 books had been read, 400 well-known actors and actresses had appeared and there had been folk tales and legends from forty-four different countries. The idea behind the programme was simple: to tell the best possible stories, of all kinds from all parts of the world, and to have them told by the best story-tellers available.

When *Jackanory* started it was quite difficult to find story-tellers who wanted to participate. No one was very interested. However, by the time of its twenty-fifth birthday, the roll-call of story-tellers was like a distinguished *Who's Who* of the British theatre: Margaret Rutherford, Wendy Hiller, James Robertson Justice, Kenneth Williams, Geraldine McEwan, Joyce Grenfell, Judi Dench, Alan Bennett, Billie Whitelaw and many, many more.

There were also people from outside the world of the theatre, especially in the late 1960s. Bob Roberts, who had been the skipper of a Thames sailing barge, told sea stories. Sir Compton MacKenzie told Greek myths and legends. Edward Ardizzone told his own 'Little Tim' stories and Eileen Cowell, a librarian and an authority on story-telling and children's literature, told English fairy tales. Wendy Wood, a fanatical Scottish Nationalist who believed in fairies and who was a wonderful natural story-teller, told Scottish traditional stories on a number of occasions. Bernard Cribbins holds the record for appearing the most times between 1966 and 1992. He took part in 111 programmes. The late Kenneth Williams followed him with 69 programmes between 1969 and 1986. Kenneth Williams' ability to create a range of varied and wonderful voices and facial expressions made him a firm favourite. He had been loath to accept the first offer he was made as he believed it involved wearing a special *Jackanory* hat.

Most *Jackanory* story-tellers used autocue, a system which allows the presenter to read the script without appearing to do so. Some purists felt that this was a kind of cheat – not real story-telling. However, fourteen minutes of text is a lot to hold in the mind – and two programmes were often recorded in one session. But some readers could not use autocue or did not wish to.

Wendy Hiller, who read Alison Uttley's 'Little Grey Rabbit' stories in the second week of *Jackanory*, was too short-sighted to see autocue. She had the script typed on jumbo type and stuck into a false book.

In the mid to late 1960s the autocue system was primitive. Words were typed in large script onto long rolls of yellow paper which were rotated below the camera lens. The reader saw only a few lines at a time and it was easy to get phrasing and punctuation wrong. Furthermore, the reader was totally reliant on the operator who rolled the script to fit the story-teller's pace. This was fine when reader and operator were in sympathy, but there were occasions when they were not and the operator might roll the script too fast – or too slowly. When the script needed to be edited for time, the yellow rolls had to be physically cut and re-spliced with transparent sticky tape. This could take a long time if there were a lot of alterations and there were days when the studio seemed to be knee deep in yellow paper. Some readers, like Kenneth Williams, went to great lengths to annotate the autocue to indicate different characters and voices. Nowadays, the system is operated electronically which makes it far easier to read and edit.

Although *Jackanory* started in a very simple style it soon became more elaborate, involving proper sets and complicated props and effects. However, the essence always remained someone telling a story. The stories were generally illustrated with drawn pictures by distinguished illustrators including Quentin Blake, Gareth Floyd and Barry Wilkinson. Sometimes film inserts were used and sometimes there were no pictures at all, for instance in the original telling of Ted Hughes' *The Iron Man* by Denholm Elliott in 1972. It was told again in 1986 by Tom Baker. In 1968 Clement Freud wrote and told a series of stories about a boy called Grimble which involved a great deal of cooking in the studio. On other occasions there were Japanese tea ceremonies and large numbers of animals, as for instance when Judi Dench told Philippa Pearce's *A Dog So Small* (1968 and 1978) and ended the story covered in a pile of puppies. Many other stories like *My Naughty Little Sister*, *Winnie-the-Pooh*, and *Mrs Pepperpot* have been told more than once.

As well as reading established stories, *Jackanory* has commissioned new work. Two memorable characters created for the programme were John Grant's Little Nose, a baby woolly mammoth, and Joan Aiken's Mortimer, a furniture-eating raven. Other characters like Joan Eadington's Jonny Briggs have spun off into series of their own. *Jackanory* has sometimes caused controversy, as when Roald Dahl's *George's Marvellous Medicine* was told by Rik Mayall in 1988. The duty office received many complaints. *George's Marvellous Medicine*, like so many of Dahl's books, is anarchic and anti-adult. It concentrates on George's attempts to get rid of his granny. The story is fantasy and very funny, especially as told by Rik Mayall, but a number of adults felt that it was both offensive and dangerous. They believed that children might be encouraged to try similar things for themselves.

This is a typical letter, received at the time:

Dear Sir
What utter tripe!! I refer to the children's programme *George's Marvellous Medicine* and what a comedown for *Jackanory*!! I understand it has been shown all week. My little granddaughter has been here hence the reason the programme was on.
Who thinks of these ridiculous programmes? Do they get paid?
It would be better to have a blank screen. We turned over to ITV and that programme *Danger–Marmalade at Work* [a comedy drama series by Andrew Davies] was just as ridiculous. I shall be writing to them.
No wonder this generation are growing up rude and odd …

The question of taste in children's television is complicated. Adults disapprove of many things children like and enjoy, and it is difficult to steer a course between pleasing the intended audience and not alienating the adult licence-payers. However, there is no doubt that, whatever adults thought about *George's Marvellous Medicine*, Roald Dahl was an outstandingly successful writer for children – and a writer whose books were actually read by the audience they were written for, not by grown-ups.

Television and reading has been an area of much discussion and debate over the years. Certainly, in the early days of television there was a fear that it would discourage reading. And certainly, when it was a novelty in the household, it may temporarily have displaced books. But there is no evidence that this happened on a long-lasting basis. However, the idea that television is to blame for problems of reading gets revived on a regular basis. In 1991, for example, the Schools Minister, Michael Fallon, held television responsible for the low standard of reading in primary schools.

There is no hard evidence of a cause or contact between television-viewing and low reading standards or a lack of interest in books. In fact, what evidence there is points in the other direction. Watching television encourages children towards books. This was always the thinking behind *Jackanory*. The producers believed that if children listened to stories being read their awareness of literature would be raised. Certainly, books which are read on television are bought and hopefully read at home. Library borrowings always rise after one has been transmitted on television. If children have enjoyed a programme they will seek out the book. As Maire Messenger Davies says in *Television Is Good for Your Kids*, 'This desire to follow up a story of which they already know the outcome in book form further suggests that children are well able to perceive the distinctions between the pleasures of television viewing and those of reading. They are different kinds of enjoyment, and one is not a substitute for the other.'

Jackanory is a great survivor and of great importance in the overall mix of BBC Children's Programmes. There have been times when it has been under pressure because of falling ratings but, well scheduled at the right time of year, it maintains a steady audience of about three million viewers and performs a great service in bringing books to children. It is a programme with a continuity of tradition; Angela Beeching, the executive producer in charge of *Jackanory* at the time of its twenty-fifth birthday, was a junior member of the production team when the programme started.

There have been other story-telling programmes on both ITV (Thames' *We'll Tell You a Story* from 1980 to 1983 and *Button Moon* from 1985 to 1988) and the BBC, notably the latter's *In the Beginning* (1970) and *The New Beginning* (1972–73). These stories from the Old and New Testaments were produced by Molly Cox, told by Ray Smith and illustrated by Graham McCallum and Paul Birkbeck of the Children's Graphics Unit. Molly Cox, who died in 1991, was, like Cynthia Felgate, an important influence in children's programming in the years after 1964. In programme terms she had two great passions: the importance of language and the spoken word, and the importance of original high-quality visuals. Despite her love of language she always maintained that television was first and foremost a visual medium. These stories combined both passions. She retold them in a way which was accessible yet maintained the Bible's richness of language, and the pictures the artists painted were equally rich and beautiful. Ray Smith, who had all the talents of the Celtic story-teller, narrated them in a truly memorable way.

Another actor who has made a name for himself as a story-teller both on BBC and ITV is Tony Robinson – possibly best known as Baldrick of *Blackadder*. He has evolved a style of dramatic, direct-to-camera story-telling shot on location against backgrounds appropriate to the action of the story. In this style, together with director David Bell, he has told the story of Theseus, made a powerful version of *The Odyssey* and a series of Old Testament stories, *Blood and Honey*, which was shot in the Holy Land. Stories like these are not easy to get across to today's audience, and too expensive to dramatize properly, but Tony Robinson's energy and conviction, plus a colloquial style of language, brings them alive and makes them accessible.

One other element of story-telling which should be mentioned is where the children themselves have an opportunity to be involved. *Jackanory* has run a number of competitions for viewers to write their own stories and poems. On each occasion there has been an enormous response. The only problem is that most younger children can only sustain writing a story over a relatively short period and the programmes therefore have to be made up of a number of short items. However, the standard of these has always been very high, and it is exciting for the child authors to have their work read by famous actors and actresses.

ITV had a similar idea in the early 1960s when Associated Rediffusion produced a programme called *Write a Play* in which two ten-minute plays written by children were transmitted. They were acted by a professional group of actors and the children involved in the production explained why they wrote the play in the way they did and what they were trying to do. Over a period of six weeks, Rediffusion received more than 10 000 plays on a wide variety of themes.

Two series called *What's Your Story?*, transmitted from Pebble Mill in 1988 and 1990, were another way of involving the audience. In the Monday programme the story-line was acted out by a cast and left open-ended. The audience was invited to phone in with suggestions for what happened next. These suggestions were co-ordinated overnight by a script editor and worked into a script, then rehearsed the next day and transmitted live that afternoon, and so on until the end of the week. They were interesting experiments and certainly provided a lot of fun for the audience, although the end results were not the highest quality drama.

Drama is the most sophisticated form of story-telling and one of the most important elements in any television schedule but it is also very expensive. BBC Radio's *Children's Hour* had a fine tradition of drama. There are few people who grew up in the 1940s and 1950s who did not thrill to the radio versions of *The Box of Delights, The Swish of the Curtain* and many others. Children's television has been transmitting drama since the department was formed – *Little Women* was broadcast in 1950–51 and *The Railway Children* in 1951 – and, as many of the producers had theatrical backgrounds, there was always great enthusiasm to increase the amount on air.

In those early days, people produced, directed, wrote and sometimes also performed. Shaun Sutton, later to be Head of the BBC's TV Drama Group, joined the Children's Department in 1952 as an 'assistant producer' to work on a seven-part adaptation of Mark Twain's *Huckleberry Finn* when the director found he had double-booked himself. At that time, there was no such job as assistant producer but it was created for the occasion. In this particular case it involved acting in the production, a tradition that was carried on. Sometimes, it meant playing more than one part. In *The Silver Swan*, in which a little girl travels through history from the Middle Ages to the Second World War, Shaun Sutton played six different characters. As he himself says: 'This idea of cheap actors led to some bad miscasting.'

Originally all the drama was done 'live' in the studio, which meant that both exterior and interior sets had to be built. Some very distinguished designers started their careers in children's television, including Eileen Diss who designed sets for the first *Billy Bunter* series in 1952. The cameras, three of them, were heavy and cumbersome and it was difficult to have a great deal of action in the studio. Soon, however, small amounts of location filming were allowed so that scenes could be set against authentic backgrounds. In 1955, when Joy Harington made her well-remembered Bible series *Jesus of*

Nazareth, she was even allowed to go location filming in Galilee. Nowadays the fashion is for nearly all drama to be shot on location, on film or video, and for the interiors to be real or purpose-built in a warehouse situation as with the adult series *Casualty*, for example, or children's television's *Byker Grove*.

Byker Grove, made by Zenith North for the BBC in Newcastle, is mainly shot in one building, once a bishop's palace and later a night-club, where the sets are permanent. Offices, make-up and wardrobe areas, canteen and tutor rooms for the children are all on hand and on one site. *Grange Hill* is made in a similar way at Elstree, in a studio used only for the programme. Today, many directors, even when they are in a studio, shoot takes out of sequence using only one camera and put the programme together in the editing suite. This technique is useful when working with children as they do not have to remember pages of script. However, some actors find the bittiness and lack of continuity irritating.

In the 1950s and early 1960s the BBC's Children's Department produced a wide variety of drama ranging from adaptations of classics like *The Black Arrow, Treasure Island, Great Expectations, Katy, The Cabin in the Clearing, Little Women* and *The Secret Garden* to specially commissioned series like *Paradise Walk, A Long Way Home* and *The Last Man Out*. It is the classics which are remembered. The tradition of the Sunday afternoon serial developed in the 1950s and was carried on by the Drama Department after

Gerald Campion, star of *Billy Bunter of Greyfriars School*, caught eating again. (BBC, 1952)

Writer and producer Joy Harington overseeing the filming of *Jesus of Nazareth* on location in Israel. (BBC, 1956)

the demise of the first Children's Department in 1964. Barry Letts, who had himself started as an actor in the Children's Department, was in charge of this slot for many years, and for a long time the Sunday classics were a way of the nation's life. They disappeared as a result of a combination of cost and fashion. Period drama of this kind is expensive to make. The casts are usually large, the actors all require costumes, wigs and make-up and the locations are expensive. *Vanity Fair*, broadcast in 1987, was one of the last serials of this kind. It was extremely costly and did not seem to appeal to the audience at which it was aimed.

From the mid-1960s, drama came under the Drama Department and little was aimed specifically at children. However, a move to revive it came out of the *Jackanory* production team. As early as 1966, I used drama inserts as a form of illustration in the programme, for Lucy M. Boston's *The Children of Green Knowe*. A small boy, Robert Wheeler, played Tolly, the hero, and was filmed in Lucy Boston's house and gardens in Huntingdonshire, the setting of the book. The core of this extraordinary house is a Norman keep inside much later additions. It is one of the oldest inhabited buildings in the United Kingdom. Many of the things described in the book were in the house and gardens and, as in the book, the birds came inside to be fed. Lucy Boston herself was a formidable woman and daunting at first meeting. She did not have a television set and was unclear about what having a television crew in the house meant. However, once she got over her first suspicion she was charming and welcoming. Everybody who was involved in that particular piece of filming remembers it clearly. There was no dialogue. Susannah York read the text over the pictures. In 1986, the BBC filmed *The Children of Green Knowe* as a complete drama serial, but at a different house.

The technique of using moving pictures as illustration was used again in Patricia Lynch's *Bookshop on the Quay* set in Dublin and Gillian Avery's *The Warden's Niece*.

The next step towards real drama was in 1968 when Nina Bawden's story *The Witch's Daughter* was illustrated with full-scale dramatized inserts with dialogue. Like *The Children of Green Knowe*, it was shot in a real location, this time on the Isle of Mull. This was not a success, largely due to my lack of experience in directing drama and the practical problems, which were enormous. A large part of the action took place in a tidal cave at the bottom of a steep cliff. Arrangements had to be made to get small children and heavy equipment in and out of the cave between the tides. The cameraman was not used to drama or children, and one of the actors had a heart attack during filming. Some of the end product was salvaged but it was not a great start. However, despite the disasters, *The Witch's Daughter* paved the way for the restart of drama made specifically for children. Head of the Children's Department, Monica Sims, was determined that it should happen and George Ageros, the departmental manager, created a budget out of nowhere.

I went to the north-east to film Catherine Cookson's *Joe and the Gladiator* in 1970. It was shot entirely on location in South Shields and Newcastle, in the streets and shipyards where Catherine Cookson had grown up. The making of the serial was fairly amateur. The production team doubled as wardrobe and design and learned about drama as they went along. However, the cast was strong. It included James Garbutt as the old rag-and-bone man and there was a real rag-and-bone man's horse, called Peggy. At this time, Catherine

The Witch's Daughter, with Helena Gloag as Annie MacLaren and
Fiona Kennedy as Perdita. (BBC, 1971)

Cookson was probably better known for her children's books than her adult ones. Another of her children's novels, *Our John Willie*, which involved a spectacular pit disaster, was successfully serialized in 1980.

In the BBC, once a reasonably successful precedent has been set it tends to continue with similar projects. This is what happened with the Children's Department's drama output. Serials, mainly adaptations from novels, became a regular part of the schedule in the early 1970s and eventually were even given proper budgets. *Joe and the Gladiator* was followed by Walter Macken's *Island of the Great Yellow Ox* adapted and directed by Marilyn Fox.

Dorothea Brooking returned to the Children's Department in 1972 to direct Noel Streatfeild's *Thursday's Child* and, later, a number of other serials. The last one she directed in her very distinguished career was for me at TVS in 1981: *The Haunting of Cassie Palmer* by Vivienne Alcock. Dorothea

Joe and the Gladiator, with Dennis Lingard as Joe, Sheila Whitmill as Anna and Peggy as 'The Gladiator'. (BBC, 1971)

Brooking was one of the most influential makers of drama from the early 1950s onwards. Generations of children have grown up on her versions of classic novels.

Another memorable adaptation relatively early on was Nina Bawden's *Carrie's War* (1974). Juliet Waley played Carrie and Rosalie Crutchley was the adult lead. It was directed by Paul Stone, who headed the Children's Drama Unit from 1981 to 1988 and produced C.S. Lewis's *The Chronicles of Narnia*. Although the original idea had been to serialize existing novels, specially commissioned material was included quite early on. Dramas were commissioned from established children's novelists like Helen Cresswell, Peter Dickinson and Bernard Ashley, as well as from relative newcomers to the genre like Richard Cooper. A drama lecturer at a teacher training college in Newcastle, Richard Cooper had written an exciting serial, *Quest of Eagles*, which had been transmitted by ITV's Tyne Tees Television in 1979, and was then commissioned by the BBC to write *Codename Icarus* (1981). He later

The children being evacuated during *Carrie's War*. (BBC, 1974)

wrote *Knights of God* for TVS. This was an ambitious and far-seeing serial which deserved greater exposure than it got. Today, the policy of the Children's Drama Unit is to keep a balance between adaptations and originals, and between period and contemporary. Period drama is very expensive, but there are important children's classics which should continue to be made. The books of E. Nesbit, Frances Hodgson Burnett and Noel Streatfeild are examples. And it is important that children should get some element of historical perspective within their drama.

Co-production and international exploitation is sometimes the answer to the money problem. BBC Enterprises do invest in children's drama – in some cases, as with *The Chronicles of Narnia*, in a major way – but projects that are suitable for this kind of exploitation are fairly limited. Ordinary, small-scale period dramas such as Gillian Avery's *A Likely Lad*, broadcast in 1992, do not attract much excitement in the international market-place. Nevertheless, it should be possible to continue to make them. It would be only too easy, under economic pressure, for children's drama to degenerate into a few, long-running, successful contemporary series and lose the richness that has traditionally been in the mix.

In 1988, the BBC Children's Department regained the Sunday afternoon slot for the transmission of *The Lion, The Witch and The Wardrobe*, the first part of *The Chronicles of Narnia*. It had taken the BBC a long time to acquire the rights to C.S. Lewis's books – doing so involved a number of people and organizations, including an American Episcopalian Church Foundation – but perhaps this was no bad thing. It meant that, by the time the rights were finally acquired, technology had evolved far enough to make a convincing production practical. Paul Stone, the producer, had already pioneered many of the techniques used in the series in his 1984 production of John Masefield's *The Box of Delights*, which involved a considerable amount of fantasy and featured a splendidly villainous Robert Stephens as Abner Brown. Marilyn Fox directed *The Lion, The Witch and The Wardrobe* and Alex Kirby *Prince Caspian/The Voyage of the Dawn Treader* and *The Silver Chair*.

The creation of Aslan, the lion, was crucial. He had to be believable and to have the power and spirituality that the character has in the books. Obviously, some of these qualities came from the voice, which was that of Ronald Pickup, but the creature himself was equally important. He was larger than life-size and extremely complicated, involving two people inside the lion and one outside and very complex electronics.

Considerable use was made of animation and many other video effects to make the magic world of Narnia. On the whole they worked well, but this kind of programme inevitably suffers when it is compared with the amazing, and amazingly expensive, special effects created for feature films. The audience has high expectations which it is not always possible to satisfy.

It is, perhaps, salutary to remember that in 1963 Pamela Lonsdale at Associated Rediffusion did a production of *The Lion, The Witch and The Wardrobe* that was made entirely in the studio and done very simply indeed. At the time it had a real impact on the audience. The BBC's *The Chronicles of Narnia* was adapted by Alan Seymour; Associated Rediffusion's by Trevor

Preston, who did a great deal of work for the Children's Departments of Associated Rediffusion and Thames in the 1970s. He went on to become a successful and hard-hitting adult dramatist.

In the late 1950s and early 1960s ITV did not feature much real children's drama. Instead, it relied on successful commercial series like *The Adventures of Robin Hood*. There was much more activity in the early 1970s with *Catweazle*, Richard Carpenter's comedy fantasy from London Weekend Television about an eleventh-century wizard trapped in the twentieth century,

Richard Greene, star of *The Adventures of Robin Hood*, welcomes a new Maid Marian, played by Patricia Driscoll, to the cast. (ATV, 1957)

Follyfoot: Gillian Blake as Dora and Steve Hodson as Steve. (Yorkshire TV, 1971)

Stacy Dorning as Jenny with Black Beauty in *The Adventures of Black Beauty*. (LWT, 1972)

Yorkshire's *Follyfoot* and LWT's *The Adventures of Black Beauty*. Southern Television tended to make children's drama that was more in the style of the BBC, with adaptations of Joan Aiken's *Midnight is a Place* and BB's *Brendan Chase* as well as *Worzel Gummidge* and *The Flockton Flyer*.

Fantasy is an important element in children's fiction, and also in children's television drama. It comes in various forms. A number of the best writers for children excel in fantasy, some of which has translated well to the screen. A memorable version of Alan Garner's *The Owl Service* was made by Granada in 1969. Helen Cresswell has written both for the BBC (*Lizzie Dripping* in 1973 and 1975 and *Moondial* in 1988) and for ITV (Central's *The Secret World of Polly Flint* in 1987). Her work is interesting because the fantasy is firmly rooted in place and therefore particularly appropriate for the screen. *Lizzie Dripping* was set and filmed in Helen Cresswell's own village of Eakring and *Polly Flint* in the nearby Rufford

The Secret World of Polly Flint: Katie Reynolds as Polly and Brenda Bruce as Granny Porter. (Central TV, 1987)

Park. *Moondial* was set in Belton House in Lincolnshire and the story centres on a sun/moondial that exists there.

Helen Cresswell remembers that as a child she loved books like the Arthur Ransome stories, which were set in real places and contained maps that the reader could follow. There are maps in the *Polly Flint* and *Moondial* books and readers can visit real places which they have seen on the screen. Incidentally, some Arthur Ransome stories have been dramatized for children's television – most notably *Coot Club* and *The Big Six* which were made by the BBC Drama Department in 1984. Ransome, rather like Enid Blyton in the *Adventure* series, suffers from being neither truly period nor modern. It is difficult for writers and actors to know whether to retain the language and accent of the period or try to update it. Neither the Arthur Ransome dramatizations nor the Enid Blyton ones were particularly successful.

Helen Cresswell makes much use of the voice-over technique:

I believe part of *Lizzie Dripping*'s great success was the use of voice-over. This is one of the few ways you can get directly into a child's mind. Children in real life are constantly pretending, saying what they think grown-ups want rather than what they are really thinking. Using voice-over they can be critical and subversive. If they said aloud some of the things they think, they would appear unattractive and rude. It would be unconvincing anyhow. As an alternative to voice-over as a way to show what is really going on in a child's mind, I use the dog Baggins for Polly to talk to and the device of telling her story into a tape-recorder for Minty in *Moondial*.

The voice-over is a perfectly respectable dramatic device which is, after all, simply a more subtle form of the time-honoured aside or monologue and, if skilfully used, can be quite unobtrusive. This or its equivalent is almost always necessary in the kind of drama I write, which depends more on the character of the central figure than on mere plot.

Some people find this technique irritating and it can be used to hide shortcomings in the script or limits to the budget. However, in Helen Cresswell's case the use is a creative and positive one.

The transmission of *Moondial* in 1988 raised the kind of problems that are often associated with fantasies which involve the supernatural and the world of magic and witches. There is a body of opinion which feels that this kind of subject matter is unsuitable for children, leading them towards the dangerous side of the occult. There have even been cases where authors have been asked to omit the word 'witch' from the title of their books. Certainly, the BBC received letters of protest about *Moondial* and, indeed, when *Blue Peter* celebrated Hallowe'en in the traditional manner. It seems ludicrous that children should be denied this world of fantasy with its age-old exploration of good and evil. Fairy tales and ghost stories are part of our literary, and therefore our television, tradition and an important part of growing up. This thesis is convincingly argued in Bruno Bettelheim's book *The Uses of Enchantment*.

Another of the BBC's fantasy dramas which explored the occult was *Moon Stallion* in 1978, an original screenplay by Brian Hayles. It was set and filmed

Sian Phillips as
Queen Boudicca in
The Warrior Queen.
(Thames TV, 1978)

in and around the Vale of the White Horse in Berkshire, a very ancient part of England. Filming there at night, in ancient burial places, quietened even the most cynical film crew. Some series do create this kind of atmosphere. Ruth Boswell who produced *The Warrior Queen* (1978), a lavish historical series about Boudicca, for Thames says this had the same kind of feeling. It was an ambitious project which starred Sian Phillips as the queen. The world of Roman Britain was created on location and one of the advising archeologists, who spent a night in the reconstructed Celtic hut, reckoned he saw Celts that night. On another occasion, when they were filming the burning of London using a model, they went off to lunch and came back to find that their own office had burnt down!

Another important series that Ruth Boswell produced for Thames was *The Tomorrow People* by Roger Price, broadcast from 1973 to 1979. It was fantasy in science fiction form, with the young protagonists 'teleporting' through

The Tomorrow People: (left to right) Peter Vaughan-Clarke (Stephen), Elizabeth Adare (Elizabeth), Dean Lawrence (Tyso) and Nicholas Young (John). (Thames TV, 1975)

space and time in a constant battle against evil forces. *Man Dog* (1972) which the BBC commissioned from the award-winning children's writer, Peter Dickinson, was also science fiction. The serial involved a dog being given the mind of a man from the future – a part that called for superdog acting skills from the canine star 'Ben'. Unluckily, after the script, which involved a considerable amount of action in a boat on a river, had been written he was found to have an aversion to boats.

The Changes (1975) was a serial based on a trilogy also written by Peter Dickinson. It required considerable adaptation as each novel was self-contained and concentrated on different characters. As the adapter, I also felt that although the final denouement worked in literary terms it did not work dramatically. The original three books were fairly radically changed. The alterations were made in close consultation with Peter Dickinson. Authors are not always so co-operative with adapters, but he accepted the fact that he was not an expert in television technique and was happy to approve the changes, provided the essence of the story was maintained. The series was set in a post-holocaust Britain that had reverted to medievalism, a world in which machines were wicked. It was an ambitious series which involved, among other things, a small army of Sikhs trekking across country, a chase down a canal and final scenes shot deep underground in Clearwell Caves in the Forest of Dean.

The Tomorrow People and *The Changes* have, like the BBC's *Dr Who*, become part of the science fiction cult world, discussed at conferences and seminars. *Dr Who* is a subject on its own and is not strictly part of this history. It was never produced by the Children's Department although it was watched by many generations of children – often from 'behind the sofa'.

Death, like magic, is an emotive area in children's programming. Many adults feel that it is not a proper subject for tea-time television, or that if it does occur it should be only in period drama in a traditional deathbed scene. But children have to experience death at some time and it is not a subject which should be ignored. In 1988 *White Peak Farm*, adapted from the book by Berlie Doherty, dealt sensitively with the subject. The character 'Danny' died in *Grange Hill*. The documentary series *Ipso Facto*, broadcast from 1989, included a whole programme on death and its taboos. In many ways children are more willing than their parents to discuss such subjects.

The BBC's children's drama has not neglected contemporary, everyday life. In the 1950s, there were several series intended to reflect real life including *The Appleyards* and *The Thompson Family*, an original series written by Noel Streatfeild. *Paradise Walk*, a four-part serial, written and produced by Shaun Sutton in 1961, dealt in a hard-hitting way with the colour problem and teenage vandalism. One of the teenagers, the bad guy, was shot and killed in the last episode. Bernard Ashley's *Running Scared*, directed by Marilyn Fox in 1986, also dealt with racism and aroused comment for its realism. The difference between the two series is not the subject matter or the message, but the style in which they were made. *Paradise Walk* was made almost entirely in the studio, *Running Scared* all on location. The development first of location filming and, later, of location video-shooting, gave a new dimension to all drama but particularly to that for children where action and pace are always important.

A number of drama series, as well as drama serials, have tried to deal with contemporary issues in a fictional context. They include *Grange Hill* (BBC),

Press Gang (Central), *Children's Ward* (Granada) and *Byker Grove* (Zenith North for the BBC). *Grange Hill* was the first of the genre.

In 1976 I was in charge of the BBC children's drama output and looking for a series that would reflect contemporary school-life rather than the traditional worlds of *Bunter* and *Jennings*. Phil Redmond was a young writer working mainly in comedy who came to talk about that and went away to create *Grange Hill*. It was not originally intended to be a long runner, but it became obvious that it was filling a great need and could be constantly renewed. In 1992, it reached its fifteenth year.

The programme's first star was Todd Carty (Tucker Jenkins) who many years later turned up as Mark Fowler in *EastEnders*. Other actors who graduated from *Grange Hill* to become names include Rudi Davies (*A Sense of Guilt*) and Susan Tully (*EastEnders*). Colin Cant was the original director of *Grange Hill* and it was he who set the style. The programme's aim was always entertainment first, but entertainment with a hard core. Over the years it has

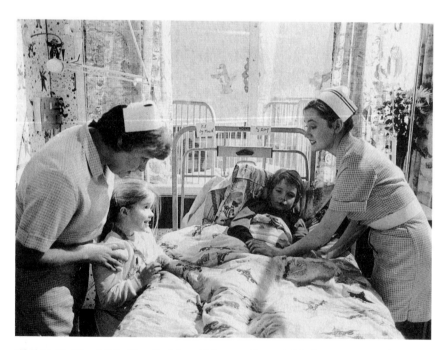

Children's Ward: Rita May (left) and Margery Bone (right) as nurses, and Emily Oldfield and Richard Hartley as the young patients. (Granada, 1990)

Press Gang starring Julia Sawalha as Lynda Day and Dexter Fletcher as Spike. (Central TV, 1992)

dealt with bullying, dyslexia, drugs, child abuse and teenage pregnancy. It has always been controversial because it showed school and teachers warts and all. But it has always maintained that it takes a clear moral stance and explains the consequences of actions.

Other series with similar objectives followed, using different backgrounds and different story angles. Granada's *Children's Ward* is set in a hospital and *Press Gang* (Central) has the device of a group of young people running their own newspaper. Both series have tackled difficult subjects with great integrity, and both are deservedly popular with the audience.

All these series aim at the upper end of the children's age-range, generally set at around thirteen. (It would have been nearer fifteen in the 1960s.) However, it is strongly felt that there should be drama aimed at the thirteen-plus age-group. There have been some successful attempts. *Going Out*, written by Phil Redmond for Southern Television, was about a group of school-leavers in their first days out of school. The series was directed by Colin Nutley who specialized for a while in drama for this age-range. He was also involved in *Radio* for TVS and *Anneka*, a co-production between Central and Swedish Television, which was filmed in the United Kingdom and Sweden and showed teenagers from different countries and backgrounds

Todd Carty as Tucker
Jenkins. After leaving
Grange Hill, he starred
in his own series
Tucker's Luck.
(BBC, 1983)

brought together through their love for each other. This was transmitted on prime time on ITV.

The BBC had *Tucker's Luck*, a spin-off from *Grange Hill*, and *Maggie* based on stories by Joan Lingard, a distinguished Scottish writer. In a slightly different style, there was *S.W.A.L.K.* from Thames, which looked at teenage romance, and, of course, *The Secret Diary of Adrian Mole, aged 13¾*. Although the latter was not made by a children's or youth department, it certainly appealed to the relevant age-group. One of the problems with this kind of drama is finding an appropriate place in the schedule where it will both find its audience and not shock the sensibilities of nervous adults. ITV chickened out over *Going Out* and showed it at around 11.30 p.m.

Single, one-off plays have been transmitted spasmodically over the years, usually because of the economic climate. It is obviously more cost-effective in terms of building sets and hiring locations to make a series rather than a single play. Most of the early one-offs were puppet plays.

Jackanory Playhouse, which started in 1972, was an extension of the story-telling programme. The plays transmitted under this title were mainly costume pieces, either based on fairy tales or newly created, and they were made entirely in the studio. There were also some contemporary one-offs like *Secrets, Billy Boy* and *Thief*, all of which dealt with serious subjects.

Thames created two umbrella series for single plays, *Shadows* (1978) and *Spooky* (1983), both of which dealt with ghostly and supernatural happenings. *Dramarama* (1983–89) was an initiative which exploited ITV's federal organization. It created an umbrella series with common titles and logo under which different stories could be shown and to which any company could contribute. Small organizations like Tyne Tees were able to get their first dramas on to the network through this series. It also provided a much-needed showcase for new writers and directors and a forum for experiment. TVS's *Young Person's Guides* written by Nigel Baldwin is an example.

ITV has also participated in a drama venture run by the European Broadcasting Union in which each country produces a single play which is swapped between the member countries. The dramas are made with the minimum of dialogue; the stories are told with music and pictures. Central have contributed a number of distingushed plays, mainly directed by Geoff Husson, centred on the problems of handicapped people. One of the best was *Look At Me*, a story about a deaf boy, which won a *Prix Jeunesse* in 1986.

In 1976, the BBC was involved in an earlier experiment of this kind with the Learning Corporation of America. In a series called *Stories Round the World* original half-hour plays were shot in various countries including Sri Lanka and Hong Kong. This involved using local casts and necessitated finding children who could not only act, but act in English.

There have also been one-off specials such as *Coronet Capers* (1975), a musical medley with the accent on royalty, *All Star Record Breakers* (1974–82), nativity plays, pantomimes and even operas.

In the 1970s the BBC was able to afford musicals for children. Paul Ciani directed *Smike*, a pop musical loosely based on *Nicholas Nickleby*, by Roger Holman and Simon May. Beryl Reid starred in the Mrs Squeers role. Paul Ciani also directed *Great Big Groovy Horse* based on the story of the Trojan horse. Paul Jones, Bernard Cribbins, Patricia Hodge and Julie Covington were among members of the cast. Jeremy Swan directed *When Santa Rode the Prairie*, a Christmas western starring William Rushton, who was also the

Smike, the musical version of Charles Dickens's *Nicholas Nickleby*, starring Andrew Keir (far left) and Beryl Reid as Mr and Mrs Squeers. (BBC, 1973)

writer. Ken Howard and Alan Blaikley wrote two musicals: *Orion* and *Ain't Many Angels*. The latter was done as a co-production with the Anna Scher Children's Theatre in London. These were all ambitious and expensive productions which could not be afforded in later years.

All drama is challenging to make, but children's drama is especially so. Finding and working with child actors is a specialized skill and many directors are not keen to master it. The actors come from many sources: some from full-time stage schools like Italia Conti and Corona, some from part-time organizations like the Anna Scher Stage School in north London where many of the original *Grange Hill* actors started. Anna Scher has been a strong influence on children's acting in Britain. Her methods have been adopted in workshops set up by Central Television and Harlech Television to provide children with training and fun and the television company with a pool of talent. Child actors also often come from ordinary schools and are picked out by the director as being right for the part. This involves a long process of improvisation, reading and so on. It may well be that this is the one and only time these children will act. Some child actors go on to be stars. Dennis Waterman, Billie Whitelaw and Sarah Greene are examples. Others disappear.

The hours children can work, and the amount of time they must spend being educated, are strictly controlled by the Home Office. This means that their working day is much shorter than that of adults and that the dramas therefore take longer to make and cost more.

In the 1980s there was a move to provide drama for the younger end of the audience in an attempt to counterbalance the more teenage-geared contemporary series. The BBC had *Jonny Briggs, Simon and the Witch* and *Happy Families*, an interesting series based on the picture books by Allan and Janet Ahlberg. It used stylized sets and drawn backgrounds and was made entirely in the studio. It also had a repertory of actors of different ethnic origins. Granada had *Josie Smith*, which was aimed at very young children and used extremely young children as actors.

At the time of writing there are no single plays for children. Indeed, there are not that many single plays for adults. One reason is cost – spreading costs across a number of episodes makes economic sense – but another reason is competition. A serial or, better still, a series, has time to build its audience. A single play has only one chance. In the past, it was possible to have seasons of one-off films made initially for the cinema. However, since the demise of Saturday morning cinema, largely because of the success of Saturday morning television, such films have been few and far between in Britain. Most drama specials, when they do happen, are animated. The admirable Children's Film Unit (in which children themselves participate in the film-making) does make films which are mainly transmitted on Channel 4, and the Children's Film and Television Foundation still exists – but only to help finance and develop projects, not to make them.

Eric Abrahams of Portobello Productions managed, after two years struggle, to put together a cinema/television deal for Roald Dahl's *Danny, the Champion of the World* in 1988, but it was a difficult enterprise and there is little to encourage others to follow suit. There is nevertheless a place for one-off films and television dramas to enrich the mainstream schedule and to encourage experiment.

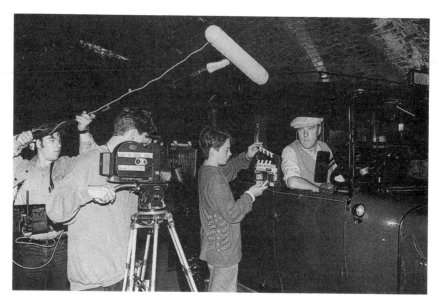

The Children's Film Unit in action filming *How's Business*. (Channel 4, 1991)

The strongest movement at present is towards long-running series and 'family drama'. The Australian series *Neighbours* and *Home and Away*, both highly popular with children, were initially made for family viewing. Series like *Degrassi Junior High*, which started life as a children's programme on the Canadian Broadcasting Corporation, is now on the air in prime time and is geared to a much wider audience. Apart from the Sunday tea-time slot, BBC Television does not really have a tradition of family drama. It may be that more thought should be given to this type of programming, but not at the expense of drama specifically geared to children. Children have a right to their own television, as much as they do to their own literature. Their emotional needs and concerns are different from those of adults, and drama is one of the best ways of satisfying these needs. It is, and should remain, a main element within the children's schedule.

CHAPTER FOUR

Information and
Specialist Programmes

Children's television has always contained a solid core of informative programmes. Programme-makers have always been aware of their responsibilities to 'educate' in the widest sense.

The magazine format has been the mainstay of children's factual programming. Magazines tend to be studio-based and hosted by presenters, and are relatively cheap. They are made up of a variety of different items with no particular theme. They are often 'live' rather than recorded, which again makes them economical: rehearsal and transmission happen in one day.

In the early days of children's television, various magazine formats combined factual material with pure entertainment items. Examples are *Telescope* (1950–51) and *Studio E* (1957–58). However, the most famous of them all is *Blue Peter*. It began in 1958 as a once-weekly, fifteen-minute programme for five to twelve-year-olds, produced by a genial eccentric called John Hunter Blair, who was known to put lighted pipes in his pockets in moments of excitement and believed that trains were for boys and dolls for girls. When it started there was nothing to indicate that this programme was going to be a long runner.

Blue Peter has been transmitted twice a week since 1964, and is probably one of the most famous children's programmes ever. It has been described as a national institution, a household word and a bastion of middle-class prejudice. A new *Blue Peter* presenter is headline news. So, too, is a good *Blue Peter* scandal, as in the 1980s when the press screamed the untrue news that Janet Ellis had been sacked for being an unmarried mother. The death of Petra, perhaps the best-known *Blue Peter* dog, in 1977 made national television news headlines. She is commemorated in a bronze statue at TV Centre where there is also a formal *Blue Peter* garden, designed by Percy

Blue Peter (BBC): (top left) The programme's first presenters: Christopher Trace and Leila Williams. (1958) (top right) John Noakes, Christopher Trace and Valerie Singleton looking at competition entries with the help of Patch the dog and Joey the parrot. (1967) (above left) John Noakes and Lesley Judd are joined by new presenter Simon Groom. (1978) (above right) Diane-Louise Jordan, John Leslie and Yvette Fielding. (1990)

Thrower who appeared in the programme from 1974 to 1988, and, since 1987, a wildlife garden. There are six *Blue Peter* lifeboats and *Blue Peter* bosses in the roof of the restored south transept of York Minster. (The full story of *Blue Peter* can be read in *Blue Peter – The Inside Story* by Biddy Baxter and Edward Barnes.)

The first presenters were Christopher Trace and Leila Williams. In 1962 Biddy Baxter became the producer of *Blue Peter*. It was she, together with Edward Barnes (later to be Head of the Children's Department) and Rosemary Gill, who really created the format of the programme which still exists today.

The involvement of the audience is one of a number of key elements in *Blue Peter*. From the start, viewers have been encouraged to write in with suggestions for items that can be done on the programme. Writers of outstanding letters receive a *Blue Peter* badge. Badges are awarded to competition winners, and children who write outstanding letters on environmental matters receive the Green *Blue Peter* Badge. There is also the prestigious Gold Badge for Outstanding Achievement. Nigel Short, the chess player, and Percy Thrower have been recipients; others have received the badge for saving lives. The programme has a unique system for filing correspondence which means that no viewer will ever receive the same reply twice.

Other important ingredients are the Makes. 'Here is one I made earlier' is now a national catch-phrase. For many years, the Makes were masterminded by Margaret Parnell. In 1963 she sent a collection of dolls' hats, beautifully made from household objects, to Valerie Singleton, who joined the programme in 1962 as co-presenter with Christopher Trace. The idea of utilizing old kitchen rubbish, toilet-paper rolls, etc. was ahead of its time in conservation terms, although there were occasional criticisms that not all viewers could afford the large quantities of sticky-backed plastic required. Conveying the idea that toys need not be vastly expensive was equally important. For instance, a Make in 1991 was a do-it-yourself Edd the Duck, who could be created far more cheaply at home than he could be bought in the shops.

Pets were an important element from 1962. The first puppy died after its first appearance on the show and, unknown to the viewers, was replaced with a look-alike whom they duly named Petra. Other famous dogs were Bonny, Honey, Patch and presenter John Noakes's Shep. 'Get down, Shep' was one of his best-known catch-phrases. Guide dogs for the blind were featured, and there was a series of cats of various kinds and temperament, some of which were seldom seen for more than a few seconds a time on the screen.

The philosophy was simple. Children are fascinated by animals, and pets are an important part of childhood. The *Blue Peter* pets were introduced to compensate the increasing number of children without gardens who could not keep pets of their own, and provided the opportunity to put over good, sound information about caring for them. (The *Play School* animals filled much the same role.) The concept of death is often introduced to children via the death of a pet and television animals have been used to introduce the subject in a relevant way.

The appeals have been another important element in *Blue Peter*. The intention has always been to get children involved directly by asking them to collect objects that could be recycled, rather than asking them for money, to give them the opportunity to help other children. Edward Barnes said it was 'like giving Christmas presents'. The appeals have varied from wool to old stamps and aluminium cans and have been amazingly successful, providing guide dogs, lifeboats, old people's centres, pure water supplies, mobile eye units ... In the past, criticism was sometimes voiced about the slightly 'do gooding' imperialist feel of some of the appeals, especially when developing countries were involved. However, there is no doubt that children are generous and compassionate and enter into appeal-collecting with huge enthusiasm.

The great advantage of a magazine format is that the programme can contain anything. A typical *Blue Peter* might have a live performance by a children's music group, a film about motor racing, an item about puppy-walking and a Make. This means that the presenters have to be very versatile. *Blue Peter* has always been live and, until quite recently, presenters performed without using autocue. They now have this aid and it reduces some of the strain. The programme has always been carefully scripted – some of the presenters felt at times that they would prefer a little more flexibility and a little less 'Biddy' speak. But the individual characters managed to shine through.

Live television has its own hazards, and many people remember Lulu, the misbehaving elephant, in 1969 and the camp fire which nearly burnt the studio down in 1971. But *Blue Peter* has to work outside as well as inside the studio. John Noakes was renowned for his exploits which included climbing Nelson's Column in London's Trafalgar Square and attempting the Cresta Run. In 1989 John Leslie marked his arrival on the programme by a spectacular display of bridge swinging: jumping off a bridge using an elasticated rope that swung him backwards and forwards under it. *Blue Peter* has always maintained a high standard of documentary film-making.

Blue Peter's woman presenters are no less adventurous. Janet Ellis achieved the record for the longest free-fall parachute jump by a civilian woman. In 1987, in her first days on the programme, Yvette Fielding was performing acrobatics with the Moscow State Circus. Being a *Blue Peter* presenter demands a great deal of dedication. The programme takes over their lives: during 1980 Tina Heath's pregnancy was charted week by week on the programme and the audience heard the heartbeat of her unborn baby during an ante-natal examination. The baby herself duly appeared in the studio less than a month after she was born.

Blue Peter has changed and evolved over the years, often motivated by the talents of the presenters. During the 1980s both Mark Curry and Peter Duncan had entertainment skills which were put to full use in a number of memorable song-and-dance routines. Simon Groom was a farmer's son, coincidentally from the farm in Derbyshire where Dorothea Brooking had filmed Alison Uttley's *A Traveller in Time*. While he was on the programme, from 1978 to 1986, there were more rural items, often filmed against the background of the farm. Biddy Baxter left the programme in 1988 having created a national institution. She was succeeded by Lewis Bronze, who says 'When Biddy left *Blue Peter*, I felt as if I had been put in charge of an institution like the British Museum. Everyone outside the business seemed to think *Blue Peter* was an institution and would last forever. To us on the programme, the first question to be answered was, "Will the programme continue?" Dropping it was certainly an option, but in the event it was not aired in front of us.' Dropping *Blue Peter* was not seriously considered for very long. Although the programme was in need of a new approach and a new look, it was basically successful and still had great potential for development.

Lewis Bronze has made a number of changes during the time in which he has been in charge. Children are now much more involved with the programme on-screen than in the past, and are treated in a more adult way. Music and arts feature more often. For instance, in 1991, during Mozart Year, a whole programme was given over to the story of the composer's life and a documentary from Salzburg. In 1990 the programme had its first black presenter, Diane-Louise Jordan.

ITV had no real challenger to *Blue Peter* until 1968 when Thames Television invited Sue Turner, whose background was in current affairs, to find the answer. The result was *Magpie*, a twice-weekly magazine which was to provide genuine competition for *Blue Peter*. It, too, was live and it was initially produced by a team whose background was outside broadcasts and current affairs rather than children's programmes. This meant they had perhaps a more journalistic approach than the *Blue Peter* production team.

Magpie was made in Thames' studios in Teddington and was transmitted as a live outside broadcast, using the studio and the surrounding lock area. The team also did many outside broadcasts from a number of other locations. Sue Turner describes them as 'postcards home'. She believes that although *Magpie* had many similarities with *Blue Peter*, including badges and appeals, its content was dominated by the presenters' point of view, whereas the content and format of *Blue Peter* was firmly controlled by Biddy Baxter. She also feels that *Magpie* was aimed at an older age-range (eight to fourteen) than *Blue Peter* and tackled subjects the BBC programme might consider unsuitable. A history series called *A Date With Tony*, which dealt with historic events in depth, is an example: the material was aimed beyond the comprehension of the younger end of the audience. There was also less emphasis on encouraging children to do things themselves.

Sue Turner played an important part in the history of ITV children's

Jon Miller and Fred Dinenage (back row), Jack Hargreaves and Marion Davies (front) say *How*. (Southern TV, 1975)

programmes. In her period *Rainbow* gained much strength and she built up a strong drama output. In the end she grew disillusioned by ITV's constant union problems and left to go farming. *Magpie* was cancelled in 1980 and, although ITV had other magazine programmes including *Splash* and *CBTV* (1983–84), there was never another real challenge to *Blue Peter*. At the time of writing, ITV has no regular information magazine.

Another ITV stalwart in the information area was *How*, a programme created by Southern Television in 1966. It was presented by Bunty James (from 1975, Marion Davies), Fred Dinenage, Jack Hargreaves and Jon Miller and was based on the simple concept of answering questions about how things worked. The presenters always greeted their audience with the American Indian 'How'. When the programme was revived by TVS in 1990, with Fred Dinenage still in place, this greeting was considered too old-fashioned and was dropped. Children's questions have been the basis for many programmes including the BBC's *Corners*. This catered for younger children and dealt with anything from how leaves grow to how spaceships work. Other similar programmes include *Search* and *Country Search* and *Tom Tom*, a children's version of *Tomorrow's World* produced in Bristol by Laurence Wade.

Programmes like *Blue Peter*, and the presenters connected with them, provide the opportunity for spin-off series. Out of *Blue Peter* came series like *Val Meets the VIPs* (Valerie Singleton), *Go with Noakes* (John Noakes) and *Duncan Dares* (Peter Duncan). It was in *Val Meets the VIPs*, a series in which Valerie Singleton invited famous people to answer questions from the child audience, that Margaret Thatcher firmly declared, in 1973, that she had no desire to be prime minister. Children are good at confounding politicians. There was a brave viewer to *Saturday Superstore* who, in 1987, pressed Mrs Thatcher firmly on her nuclear policy and was well prepared with supplementary questions.

The one-off documentary, traditionally a major element in adult schedules, has held a lesser place in children's television. Documentary feature material has tended to be included in the magazines, and single documentaries have not always proved very successful with viewers. It is often easier, and more effective, to discuss serious issues like drugs or sex within the format of drama series as has been done in the BBC's *Grange Hill*, Central's *Press Gang* and Granada's *Children's Ward*. All these programmes have dealt with drugs, teenage pregnancy, sexual abuse of children and many other similar social issues.

There have been some noteworthy documentary series over the years. Many, like Central's *This Is Me* (1983–84) and the BBC's *The Lowdown* (1988–) and *Ipso Facto* (1989–), were based on children's own experiences. There were spin-off documentaries from *Magpie* including *My Brother David*, the moving story of a deaf boy. There were also some strong stories in ITV's *Docurama* series of real-life stories and a number of *Blue Peter Special Assignments* (1973–81).

Some subject areas have been more difficult to cope with than others. There has never really been a wholly successful children's science series, and history and archaeology have been comparatively rare. However, the BBC did have a noteworthy archaeology series, *The Story Beneath the Sands*, in 1978,

'Keeper' Johnny Morris with James the orang-utan in the *Animal Magic* studio. (BBC, 1975)

produced by Molly Cox who was also responsible for two other series, *Fabulous Animals* and *Unsolved Mysteries*, and there was a lavish historical documentary series produced by Edward Barnes: *Treasure Houses*. In this, visits to famous houses were enhanced by dramatized inserts. In 1990 and 1991 the independent production company Third Eye Productions made two series of archaeology programmes for the BBC called *Now Then*. These also used a mixture of dramatized inserts and visits to actual sites, with painted reconstructions by Paul Birkbeck who made a welcome return to children's television in this series. Thames Television made *Owl TV*, a natural history programme. It was co-produced with a Canadian company which enabled both companies to share the costs.

When subjects are as specific as science, history or mathematics, it is sometimes difficult to decide what a children's schedule should provide over and above what is provided in the classroom and on Schools Television. If the programmes are too didactic the audience will reject them feeling that they are being lectured. On the other hand, there is a desire for knowledge and information and Public Service Broadcasters have always considered it their job to fulfil this need.

It is the form in which they do so that is important, and it will become increasingly so as competition develops. In the United States, the Children's Television Workshop's *3, 2, 1 Contact*, a children's science show, finds it difficult to compete with animated series. It is interesting, incidentally, to note the advent of 'green' animation series like *Captain Planet* which try to legitimize themselves by dealing with subjects of world environmental importance. The problems of putting over factual information is one of the reasons why the genre of 'factual entertainment' developed, pioneered by Johnny Ball. This is discussed in Chapter Six.

Animals and nature have always been a mainstay of children's television. Armand and Michaela Denis's *On Safari* was shown in children's time from 1957 to 1965, George Cansdale presented *All About Animals* during the 1950s (and was a contributor to *Blue Peter* from 1962 to 1988) and Sir David Attenborough made his television debut in *Zoo Quest* in 1954.

Animal Magic was transmitted from 1962 to 1983 and was one of the longest running animal series. In the early 1960s, when the success of adult natural history programmes became clear, it was decided to create one for children. Johnny Morris was already known as a children's presenter and he believed that if information was delivered in an entertaining way children would be more interested. He created the character of a zoo keeper and used his ability to create a variety of voices to bring the animal characters alive in the many films he made at Bristol Zoo.

Working with animals, as everyone knows, can be hazardous. Johnny Morris tells of the occasion when he asked whether he could take Jack, a fifteen-year-old orang-utan who lived in Bristol Zoo, for a walk along the terrace hand-in-hand. This was something his keeper Stanley often did, the two of them ending up in the keepers' restroom for lunch. It was agreed that Johnny could have a go – but that there would be only one attempt. There was no way in which Jack would perform more than once.

So Johnny went into the enclosure and Jack came to meet him. The orang-utan scrabbled a little on the floor, then stood up holding out his hand for Johnny to take. Johnny took it and was grasped firmly in that huge paw. They walked past the camera together and Jack leered smugly at his companion, clearly saying, 'Everything all right, mate?' What Jack knew, and Johnny knew by then, was that when he had scrabbled on the ground he had picked up a large dollop of something quite revolting and handed it to Johnny. It was pressed between their palms and there was nothing that could be done about it until the end of the take.

Animal Magic, despite its longevity, was very much a programme of the 1960s. As children's audiences became more sophisticated the whole idea of anthropomorphism became old-fashioned and less acceptable, and programmes with a more serious approach appeared. The first of these was *Wildtrack*, in 1978, produced by Mike Beynon. He was able to harness the expertise of the BBC's Bristol Natural History Unit, using their specialist cameramen. He also devised some bizarre competitions. One was sparked off by a postcard that purported to convey 'all the beauty and splendour of Scottish wildlife' and featured a fox and a capercaillie, a large grouse, posed together. Unfortunately, on close inspection, the fox proved to be stuffed. *Wildtrack* invited other similar contributions and was inundated.

The Really Wild Show: Chris Packham on the London Underground wearing a motorized tail to explain why animals have a tail. (BBC, 1988)

Mike Beynon also started *The Really Wild Show*, in 1986, which later evolved into *The Really Wild Roadshow* (1991). The former was a mainly studio-based programme which allowed children in the audience to be involved with animals. The style was a great deal more noisy and participatory than that of earlier series but, even so, a lot of solid information was put over. Chris Packham, Nicola Davies and Terry Nutkins were all experts in their fields and presented the show with authority. *The Really Wild Show* deservedly won a number of prizes. It had an innovative style mixing live studio film, graphics and animation to create an entertaining package of information.

However, there were problems with a studio-based programme of this nature. Often the animals would not perform to order, and small children ended up sitting in the studio for a long time waiting for something to happen. Sometimes it happened in the wrong sense, as when a studio full of rabbits being cuddled by the audience lost patience and bladder control. (Rabbits are notoriously risky. There was a group in the BBC's *Going Live!*

119

which, aroused by the lights and warmth, became extremely and embarrassingly active.)

The Really Wild Roadshow attempted to solve these problems by going on the road to places where the animals would be in more familiar surroundings. As a result, there was much more variety in the programme with large animals and birds used in a much freer way. The BBC's Children's Department has always benefited from the expertise of the specialist Natural History Unit in Bristol. Most of the people who make children's natural history programmes are part of this unit but the editorial brief comes from the Head of Children's Programmes in London. It is a system which has worked very well over the years.

The ITV company which specializes in natural history is Anglia, well known for adult series such as *Survival*. Anglia has not often made series specifically for children, although in 1980 much of its fine footage was repackaged as *Animals in Action* for a children's slot. During the 1980s TVS did a number of series with David Taylor, the zoo vet, who started in *No 73* and who then went on to appear as the visiting expert on *Talking Animal* (1984–85). Andrea Arnold, the presenter of the latter, later went on to do another, *A Beetle Called Derek*. In the 1980s awareness of environmental issues increased and so did children's concern about them. David Bellamy was

Motormouth: (back row, left to right) Tony Gregory, Caroline Hanson and Neil Buchanan; (front row) Julian Ballantyne, and Andrea Arnold. (TVS, 1988)

Vision On: (left to right) Pat Keysell, Ben Benison and Tony Hart examining another machine designed by Prof Wilf 'Makepeace' Lunn. (BBC, 1972)

connected with a number of children's programmes in this field, among them *Bellamy's Bugle*. Another leading campaigner, mainly on ITV, is Bill Oddie, a keen ornithologist and conservationist.

Programmes like BBC TV's *Blue Peter*, TVS's *Motormouth* (1989–92) and BBC TV's *Going Live!* also deal with the environment and conservation. The level of children's concern was demonstrated by the huge reaction to *The Blue Peter Green Book*, published in 1990. They have a great interest in natural history and environmental issues and get very involved.

There is always much discussion about how specialized and targeted children's programmes should be. (This also happens in adult television, especially with the greater awareness of significant minorities in the viewing public.) One part of the audience which the BBC singled out quite early on was the deaf. Ursula Eason, the long-time Deputy Head of Children's Programmes and one of the most influential and unsung heroines of children's television, was the force behind programmes specifically for deaf children.

The original series, in 1952, was called *For Deaf Children* and was worthy but somewhat ponderous. Written captions were held for long periods to enable the viewers to read the content. In 1964 Ursula Eason was joined by Patrick Dowling as director and together they revitalized the programme under the title *Vision On*. There was some sign language, by the presenter Pat Keysell, and some speech to allow children to lip read.

There are many factions in the world of the deaf child and the programme was often caught between them – lip reading versus sign language, for instance. There were also problems with holding large close-ups to enable children to lip read as this meant that they were not seeing relevant body language. After the first series of *Vision On* words were dropped completely. The programme became a visual experience to be enjoyed by all the viewers not just those who were deaf. Tony Hart joined Pat Keysell and the programme accumulated a whole team of people working in cottage industries. Animators, illustrators and mime artists were all keen to experiment with the new techniques that were developing in television. It was in *Take Hart*, in 1977, that Morph, the animated plasticine creature, made his first appearance. Technical change was fast in the late 1960s and early 1970s and there was plenty of scope to experiment.

Despite the fact that *Vision On* still had the deaf audience very much in mind, and although there were no words, sound was very important. The producers knew that many deaf children could respond to vibrations and used sound to determine the pace and mood of the show.

The idea of 'The Gallery', taken from Adrian Hill's *Sketch Club*, was developed in *Vision On*. Children were invited to send in pictures and the most interesting were shown on the programme. When it was decided to drop *Vision On* in 1976 and create a more general arts programme introduced by Tony Hart, 'The Gallery' continued as part of *Take Hart* and, from 1984, *Hartbeat*. In the 1970s more than 10,000 pictures a week were being sent in.

Tony Hart had been involved in children's television from the earliest days as a graphics artist. *Take Hart* and *Hartbeat* gave him the opportunity not only to speak, but also to develop a whole range of creative ideas which encouraged children to paint, draw and make things for themselves. It is not

We Are the Champions Special featuring disabled children. (BBC, 1985)

easy to deal with art, or the arts in general, in children's programmes. Apart from Tony Hart's series, the only other one that has really succeeded in this area is TVS's *Art Attack* hosted by Neil Buchanan. It is difficult to make looking at great pictures exciting on the small screen. One programme which did this successfully was made by the Children's Television Workshop in America when Big Bird from *Sesame Street* toured the Metropolitan Museum in New York.

The involvement of physically and mentally handicapped children in television programmes is an area of increasing concern. The only programme of this kind that the BBC has made in recent years is the annual *We Are the Champions Special*, first transmitted in 1987, in which teams of disabled children compete in a number of different games. Efforts are also made to include them in programmes like *Blue Peter* and *Going Live!* In drama, there were two disabled actors for a time in *Grange Hill*. Channel 4 has had several series aimed at children with disabilities. A 1992 *Prix Jeunesse* winner was Channel 4's *Beat That* which featured disabled children setting up a restaurant.

It is not always easy to carry out the best intentions. There was an occasion at TVS, in 1984, when Avril Rowlands had written a drama series, *Lettie*, specifically centred on a handicapped girl. There was a nation-wide search to find a girl who was handicapped, could act and was strong enough to cope with the filming. In the end it proved impossible and the part was played by an able-bodied actress, Victoria O'Keefe, who spent a great deal of time researching the physical aspects of the disability. This casting was criticized at the time, but it seemed better than not doing the drama at all. Geoff Husson used disabled actors with great success in one-off dramas for ITV: a paraplegic in *Just a Normal Girl* and a Down's syndrome boy in *Tide Race*. His aim was to raise awareness in the viewing audience and counter stereotyping.

Literature has also been a problem. The only series which attempted to tackle children's literature head-on was Yorkshire's *The Book Tower*, created by Joy Whitby. It was a long-running (1979–89), prize-winning and praise-worthy series but in a world of increasing commercial pressure sadly did not survive. Classical music has been equally difficult. Apart from any other consideration, music programmes are expensive because of the cost of the orchestras. But it is also difficult to make serious music attractive to a non-specialist child audience. There have been some brave attempts. The wonderful percussionist James Blades, the original sound of the J. Arthur Rank gong, was a welcome guest in the early days of *Play School*. In the late 1980s, the BBC attempted to mix musical genres in *What's That Noise?* to convey the idea that all music is fun. And a number of documentaries have featured musical children. On the whole, however, the tendency has been to deal with all the arts in small segments within magazine formats, where they seem more palatable.

A crucial element in adult programming is the news. However, this is a difficult genre to produce for children. Many people believe that they should be protected from the harsher realities of life. Certainly, in the 1950s there was no attempt to provide hard news for children. *Children's Newsreel* was a magazine of general interest items that featured animal stories, local customs, royal openings, etc. It was compiled from available footage and was similar in style to the *Children's Newspaper*, a rather worthy, heavygoing publication of the day. It certainly did not attempt to cover world events or political activity. It survived until 1961. For a time there was no attempt to provide a news service, although *Blue Peter* attempted the occasional current affairs feature using library footage and voice-over. A strong feeling that children were not interested in news was borne out by a survey which showed that only a tiny percentage of them ever watched adult news.

Edward Barnes, who had worked on BBC TV's *Tonight* and had a keen interest in news, often directed the *Blue Peter* features. He believed that if children were provided with news that was angled to them they would watch. The idea of a regular news programme for children was born in the autumn of 1971. Another, much more practical, issue helped to create it. At that time there were no live presenters on children's television and therefore no buffer if programmes did not run to time. A daily live programme could be adjusted in its running time to make the whole schedule work out to the proper length. Edward Barnes took the idea to Paul Fox, then Controller of BBC 1, who supported the idea and sent Barnes to talk to Derrick Amoore, Editor of TV News, who was very enthusiastic. A strange partnership grew up between the News Department and the Children's Department which has continued ever since. The editorial control of the programme is the responsibility of the Children's Department and the editorial staff belong to that department. But the programme is made in the news area, using news resources, studios, cutting-rooms, crews, etc. It is a unique set-up and one which works.

Initially, the whole idea of live children's news was seen as an experiment. There were only two programmes a week and the main concern of the production team was to establish their credibility in the eyes of their new colleagues in the News Department.

None of the production team had real journalistic experience and they therefore needed to find a presenter who had. Jonathan Dimbleby was the first choice but he declined, so John Craven was approached. He had already worked on children's programmes with Jill Roach, former researcher/director on BBC Bristol's magazine programme *Search*, and had wide

John Craven taking *Newsround* abroad to meet Thai refugees on the Cambodian border. (BBC, 1978)

experience in regional broadcasting. So *John Craven's Newsround* was born. From the start, the style was informal to distinguish it from adult news. John Craven did not wear a suit nor did he pontificate from behind a desk.

Newsround believed it had 'a mission to explain' long before that became a news and current affairs buzz-phrase. The intention was to put events in context, to explain the background and, where possible, to see things from a child's point of view. *Newsround* will cover all stories it believes are of importance and interest to its audience. Unlike *Children's Newsreel*, it has always covered hard stories including war and disasters. One of the greatest advantages the programme has is that BBC correspondents will file stories specifically for the programme. From the beginning this was a great strength, with reporters like Martin Bell reporting from Vietnam and, in the 1980s, Michael Buerk from South Africa.

It took time for *Newsround* to establish its credentials. Jill Roach says she felt that much of her job was diplomatic, keeping the balance between the Children's and News Departments and building up the programme's reputation. However, over the years it became a BBC institution and was taken seriously by the News Department. It was *Newsround* that broke the news of the Challenger shuttle disaster in 1986, and it was Eric Rowan, the editor, who had to decide very quickly indeed which pictures coming in live from CNN were suitable for use on the programme. Pictures have to be even more carefully selected for a child audience than for an adult one, but the general feeling is that children should be taken seriously and not be over-protected. Again, context and explanations are crucial. It is hoped that if a child sees the story in the adult news, presented in a slightly different way, he or she will understand more of what that news is about.

There have been occasions when there has been conflict between the Children's Department and the News Department over introducing news flashes within children's time (4.50–5.35 p.m.). The News Department understandably wishes to get its headlines on air before its competitors. The Children's Department equally understandably wishes to maintain its schedule and to introduce the news in its own way via *Newsround.* There is a general understanding that, all things being equal, there should be no news flashes within the children's period and the news should be broken in *Newsround's* 5 p.m. slot. If this is not possible or appropriate the news flash should go to BBC 2. There will no doubt be occasions when this unwritten understanding will be challenged, but on the whole it works well for both audiences.

Over the years *Newsround* has taken up a number of issues of particular interest to children. It gave a great deal of coverage to the emergence of the green movement and to the activities of organizations like Friends of the Earth, which did not feature prominently in adult bulletins in their early days. Under Eric Rowan's editorship *Newsround*, together with *Grange Hill*, was associated with the 'Just Say No' campaign against drugs and also with the activities of Childline.

In news, as much as in drama, there are subjects that are difficult in terms of a child audience. They tend to centre round the same issues: violence and sexual matters. Violence can be addressed through careful picture selection and in the way stories are handled, but there will often be complaints. For example, in 1991, when film relating to allegations about the activities of the Quorn Hunt was shown there were no close-ups. It did include long shots of foxes being torn to pieces. The feeling of the production team was that any child out for a walk in the country could have seen these scenes and that it therefore was valid to show them. However, there was considerable protest and the case was taken to the Broadcasting Standards Council.

The complainant considered that, with no advance warning, the use of the material the *Newsround* sequence contained, showing scenes of foxes and hounds, was uncaring and tasteless at a time when many children would be watching. After viewing the sequence and reading the BBC's statement the Complaints Committee judged as follows:

> In the view of the Complaints Committee the choice of shots used in the item was carefully made and the accompanying commentary was drafted with equal care having in mind the audience at which the programme was aimed. It recommended that the complaint should not be upheld.

There were also problems during the first National Aids Week in 1988. This was clearly a news event, but traditionally children's television did not discuss the sexual act, either heterosexual or homosexual. Originally *Newsround* decided to ignore it, but were overruled on the grounds that children could not fail to be aware that Aids Week was happening. The programme concentrated on the aspects that were likely to scare children, calming fears that they might catch the disease from lavatory seats or swimming-pools or kissing. In this instance the programme did a sensible job, demystifying a complex subject. How to deal with questions like this is a constant problem for the editor of *Newsround* and, indeed, the Head of the Children's Department. The rules about what is acceptable at five o'clock in the afternoon change all the time, and there must be a constant awareness of where the lines are drawn.

John Craven stayed with *Newsround* until 1989 and edited it himself for the last three years. His association with the programme was so great that many people referred to it as *John Craven's Newsround* even after he had left. However, the presenters who succeeded him have established their own style, although without being identified with the programme in the same way.

Newsround continues to attract a sizeable audience of children, and also of adults who find that the programme's simplicity and straightforwardness provides a good background to the news.

ITV never managed to establish a children's news service, although Thames was at one stage very keen to do so. There have also been attempts in other parts of the world, but the programmes are mostly current affairs magazines rather than true news services. At the time of writing there are three other daily news programmes for children in Europe: in Holland, Austria and Germany. All acknowledge the example of *Newsround*. *Newsround* has proved that children will watch news if it is provided in a palatable and non-patronizing way, and if it is carefully scheduled between programmes they are keen to watch.

A number of programmes developed from *Newsround*, including *Newsround Extra*, a series of mini-documentaries that are filmed all over the world and deal with a wide variety of subjects.

During his editorship, Eric Rowan started the idea of a children's election run in parallel with the General Election and centred on schools in the various constituencies. The first one was held in 1983 and over 100,000 children took part, writing their own manifestoes, making their own speeches and casting their own votes. On that occasion the children of Britain voted the same way as their parents. In 1989, they triumphantly voted the Green Party to power, and in 1992 their vote was Labour 26.8 per cent, Conservatives 25.4 per cent and Liberal Democrats 23 per cent.

News has played a part in Saturday morning programming, although not on as regular a basis as *Newsround*. John Craven contributed news slots to various programmes and, at the time of writing, Juliet Morris is covering stories of particular interest to children on *Going Live!* with more in-depth discussion and debate than is possible on *Newsround* itself. The first topic was a discussion of the pros and cons of boxing in the light of Michael Watson's injury in 1991.

CHAPTER FIVE

Saturday Mornings

Children's Saturday cinema was still an established ritual during the 1960s and early 1970s and the idea of a network Saturday morning television sequence for children only really started in 1976, when the BBC's *Multi-Coloured Swap Shop* was invented. (*Tiswas* started in 1974 but only in the ATV region.) Before that Saturday mornings were a mixture of old movies, bought-in programmes, cartoons and the occasional original series. The BBC series tended to be entertainment orientated with programmes like *Whoosh!* (1968), *Zokko!* (1968-69) and *Ed and Zed* (1970). *Zokko!* was interesting in that it had no live presenters. The various items were fitted to a pre-recorded sound-track and linked by graphics. On ITV, Gerry Anderson's space puppet series were important elements in building the Saturday morning schedule.

Swap Shop was originally planned as a series of six programmes. It ended up as 146 and was a breakthrough. It was the first time that Saturday morning had been thought of as a different kind of programme slot – a time when children were likely to be more relaxed than during the week, a time for television to be out and about. It was also recognized that the audience might well switch in and out of the programme because of other activities, and that it therefore could not be assumed that every viewer would watch the whole programme.

The first producer of *Swap Shop* was Rosemary Gill, who had worked on a number of children's programmes including *Blue Peter*. Her idea of swapping as a basis for the show was simple but very clever.

> I thought the idea of swapping was a good one because I remembered I was always swapping things as a child at school. Swapping is more than just a swap of a mouth-organ for a dinky toy, it is a swap of information.

Originally *Swap Shop* was planned to be fairly small scale with a presenter in the studio who would link items for three hours. However, this became claustrophobic and outside broadcasts were introduced. Because the programme went out in winter, soccer or rugger outside broadcast teams were always out on Saturdays and they were used for *Swap Shop* in the mornings. Children were extremely enthusiastic about participating in the broadcasts and would flock to the venue as soon as it was announced. They often arrived half-dressed and wearing odd shoes. The only problem with these outside broadcasts was that the sites tended to be wide and windy open spaces and there were often a lot of very cold, blue-looking participants.

Rosemary Gill was determined that *Swap Shop* should be completely different in feel and style from *Blue Peter*. One of the principal innovations was the 'phone-in', which created the first real access programme for children and became the mainstay of this kind of programming. It had already been tried in 1975 in a BBC children's programme called *Z Shed* whose presenter, Noel Edmonds, became the presenter of *Swap Shop*. He hosted *Swap Shop* in the studio, guests dropped in and there were the usual animal items, competitions, etc. Because Noel was the sole presenter, it was decided that he needed a character to work off and Posh Paws, a purple dinosaur, joined him on the show. There was also the invisible 'Eric'. He did not exist, but was supposed to lurk somewhere in the roof and lower bundles of cards and letters to the studio floor. People swore that they saw him! Eric gave his name to the *Swap Shop* Star Awards that were awarded to performers and programmes as a result of the audience's vote. Keith Chegwin was the presenter of the outside broadcasts. When he was nineteen, he wrote in to the BBC saying that he had always wanted to be a children's presenter and that he had been in the business for ten years and had lots of ideas. Could he come in and talk? Rosemary Gill thought cheek of this kind was worth a try and took him on after one interview. On a later outside broadcast in Bruges in Belgium Keith Chegwin and co-presenter Maggie Philbin got engaged.

Swap Shop broke new ground and took many risks. At first the technical people were concerned that broadcasting a virtually unrehearsed, quite complicated programme live might result in a decline in standards. But they all wanted it to work and, over the years, co-operation between the technical

Multi-Coloured Swap Shop: Keith Chegwin and Noel Edmonds opening up the phone lines. (BBC, 1976)

and the creative production teams was always excellent. This co-operation continued as the programmes became more complicated, and as other series like *Saturday Superstore* (1982-87) and *Going Live!* (1987–) evolved. There was one occasion on the former when the pop group Bucks Fizz was supposed to appear in a live outside broadcast tramission from Jersey. Two of the group had arrived there on the Thursday and the other two were supposed to follow them on Friday. However, the airport on the island was fogbound and, after circling for some time, they had to return to London. The engineers managed to put the group together using a technique called CSO (colour separation overlay). The singers in Jersey played on an open-air stage in Royal Square, the other two against a special blue background in the studio in London. The engineers were able to join the two sets of pictures together and it looked as though all four were all performing in the same place.

The outside broadcasts continued for a long time but were eventually dropped as a regular Saturday morning ingredient when *Going Live!* started. So many children turned up to take part in them that safety became a problem and the participants had to be corralled behind barriers. Eventually, outside broadcasts became scream and shout affairs. It was decided that the open-air anti-claustrophobic element of the programme could be achieved in a different way, by making a number of short films, and it would only be sensible to have an outside broadcast if it was a major happening. The occasion when the programme crossed the Channel by ferry in real time is one example. Another is when it was transmitted from a train on the Watercress Line, an old steam railway in Hampshire. This was a real feat of engineering skill involving satellite links and helicopters.

Saturday Superstore, presented by Mike Read, had many of the same ingredients as *Swap Shop* although there was initially an attempt to give it a vague story-line: the presenters had roles connected with the store and appeared in certain departments. There was a period when David Icke ran the Sports Department, and Sarah Greene first appeared as 'The Saturday Girl'. However, this idea was more or less dropped after the first series.

Going Live! took over from *Saturday Superstore* in 1987. Phillip Schofield, who had established himself as an accomplished and popular presenter on Children's BBC, joined Sarah Greene as co-presenter. Again, the programme followed the basic *Swap Shop* formula: it was live with phone-ins, guests, pop – a lot more than in the early days of *Swap Shop* – competitions and children in the studio. There were also new ingredients. A comedy element was introduced with Trevor and Simon, who were encouraged to create short sketches to punctuate the show.

There was also a definite move to include more serious items and to involve children as much as possible in the programme. In earlier shows the children, particularly those in the studio, had sometimes seemed more like set dressing than real people. New items such as 'Soap Box' in which children speak out on issues or 'All About Me', a strand in which children talk about their lives, were introduced. 'Growing Pains', hosted by Phillip Hodson, the agony uncle, allowed the programme to deal with subjects as difficult as child abuse and Aids.

When the content of a programme is as varied as this, it requires very skilled presenters who can change its gear and tone without seeming awkward. Chris Bellinger, editor of *Saturday Superstore* and, later, *Going*

Live!, who worked on all the BBC winter Saturday morning shows, believes that the advent of the earpiece, which enables the producer to talk directly to the presenter on air and steer them when necessary, has helped this kind of problem. The Saturday morning shows do not use autocue.

ITV's best-known Saturday morning show was probably *Tiswas*, made by ATV. It was hosted by Chris Tarrant, who was originally a serious news reader on ATV's regional news programme *Today*. He was involved in an early experiment for a programme that took place in a small presentation studio with just a handful of staff. Letters were invited and competitions started. The programme started in 1974 as a regional series in Birmingham. The first producer was Peter Harris, who coined the title *Tiswas* (Today it's Saturday wear a smile). He felt it evoked the chaos and pandemonium suffered by the production team as the programme went out live. *Tiswas* became so popular that in 1979 it transferred to the whole network using a proper-sized studio and with a proper budget. It was billed in the *TV Times* as follows:

> If you want culture, education, serious discussion and politics you won't find it here. But if you want slapstick, cartoons, animals, pop stars and hundreds nay millions of – well two or three anyway – hysterically funny jokes then this is the space to watch.

Chris Tarrant eventually had to give up his news-reading job. It was thought to be inconsistent that he read serious news about a car crash on Friday night and appeared on Saturday morning with a bucket on his head!

Tiswas was a deliberately anarchic show. Water was thrown around from early in the series. (Inevitably, there was a union dispute about who handled the bucket and who threw the water.) One of the co-presenters, along with Sally James, was Lenny Henry who was very young and who had first come to attention through the talent show *New Faces*. It was during the run of *Tiswas* that he started creating characters like Razzamatazz and the David Bellamy character. The anarchic, messy nature of *Tiswas* was an antidote to the rather more staid BBC programmes. There were items like 'The Phantom Flan Flinger' and 'Flan Your Folks'. The whole programme was very anti-adult and on the side of the audience. In the end, it got out of hand and appealed more

Chris Tarrant (left) and Sally James who bought chaos to Saturday mornings with *Tiswas*. (ATV, 1979)

to a cult adult audience than to children and eventually, for this reason, it was taken off in 1982. However, by that time 'gunge' had become an integral part of children's television.

The story-line concept which appeared briefly in *Saturday Superstore* occurred in other Saturday morning programmes. Granada's *The Mersey Pirate* (1979) and *Fun Factory* (1980) are examples. The former took place on a real boat, manned by characters that included two comic stowaways whose material was written by Alan Bleasdale. The complications of operating a programme at sea meant that it was not really practical. *Fun Factory* came from an old warehouse in Manchester. Jeremy Beadle played the factory's Research and Development Officer and there were strands like 'Canteen Cabaret' in which children did their own acts.

The programme which took the idea of a story-line furthest was *No 73* from TVS who in 1980 won the franchise for the South of England from Southern Television. One of their aims was to make a mark in children's programmes. I had left the BBC to join the franchise group and create a children's department. TVS decided that Saturday morning was a good target.

No 73 opens its door to Saturday mornings: (from left to right) Pat Doyle, Andrea Arnold (on car), Nick Staverson (in front) and Sandi Toksvig. (TVS, 1982)

We were very interested in the possibility of creating live drama and we had a team including the director, Nigel Pickard, who were able to put this into practice. TVS was a regional company with no automatic access to the ITV network, so the first two series of *No 73*, in 1982, only went out in the TVS area, where it replaced *Tiswas* – much to the disgust of that programme's fans who picketed the studios. It was networked from 1983. John Dale, who had worked in the theatre and in children's television at the BBC, created the format and soon became the producer. With his background in theatre, he worked from the basis of character and place. He wanted to create an adult world into which the audience was invited on Saturday morning.

No 73 was a house inhabited by a non-nuclear family. Ethel, played by Sandi Toksvig, was an aunt rather than a mother figure and the other characters – Dawn who always moved on roller-skates, Harry the dim one and Neil – all fitted into the household. The traditional Saturday morning guests fitted into the ongoing story-line, which often involved the neighbours and other regulars. So Gary Glitter would be interviewed in the kitchen and live bands played in the living-room. The script was developed through improvisation and an intensive rehearsal period, and the actors had considerable creative input. It was an original and daring programme and was recognized as such when it went on the network. However, it also had its problems. It was extremely time-consuming to make as it involved outside rehearsal in London and the whole of Friday on the set in Maidstone. Because TVS was new and not using its studios a great deal, the very expensive sets could be left standing all week to make this possible. Other Saturday morning programmes had never had this luxury.

In 1988, TVS started *Motormouth* to compete with *Going Live!*. In a thesis written for the Polytechnic of Central London, Sally Turner compares the two programmes.

She describes the difference in rhythm and length of items:

The TVS show works on a much faster rhythm than *Going Live!* because the programme has to work around commerical breaks which split the show into twenty-minute slots. *Motormouth 2* will spend an average six or seven minutes on an item whereas *Going Live!* will spend ten or twelve minutes . . .

An example of this was when both programmes did a programme on the Walt Disney film *Honey, I Shrunk The Kids* – Nigel Pickard, the executive producer, explains: '*Motormouth* spent four and a half minutes on the subject whereas *Going Live!* spent thirteen minutes on it and produced a far more detailed and interesting feature. They did behind-the-scenes interviews and talked about the special effects . . . We tend to do tasters, we say there is a good film, say why it is a good film and leave it at that.'

Sally Turner goes on to talk about the style of presentation, and again quotes Nigel Pickard: '*Motormouth* is far more anarchic than *Going Live!*, not anarchic for anarchy's sake but we are more visually and verbally exciting. We take more risks.'

Sally Turner continues:

Certainly the programme is visually exciting and has a very instant appeal. The short informative features do not require a lot of concentration from the viewers. *Going Live!*'s slower pace and attention to detail requires viewers to pay attention more closely and for longer periods but its features are more interesting because of this approach. This is perhaps one of the reasons why *Going Live!* is the more popular of the two programmes. In ratings terms the BBC programme has beaten *Motormouth* every week since the two series began.

Live Saturday morning programmes have an atmosphere and tension all their own. The feeling in the production gallery before going on air is one of excitement and muted hysteria. There was a period in the history of *Going Live!* when everyone in the gallery used to do a kind of war-dance before the programme started. Live television is always exciting and always dangerous. In *No 73* terms, it was even more dangerous because of the drama element: it mattered if the set fell down. Another problem was that the actors found it difficult to retain their characters while doing straight interviews. (This problem has occurred again in the independent production *Parallel 9* made by Roach and Partners for the BBC in summer 1992.) Despite workshops in interviewing, there were often uncomfortable gear changes. However, on the whole the programme was a success; it had energy, and a more controlled

Saturday Superstore: Keith Chegwin taking part in the annual River Raft Race at Stratford-upon-Avon, with the team from Wellesbourne and District Lions Club. (BBC, 1984)

Sarah Greene and Phillip Schofield and fashion expert Annabel Giles launching *Going Live!* with the help of Gordon the Gopher. (BBC, 1987)

anarchy than *Tiswas* that made it a real alternative to the BBC's offerings. By the time its run ended in 1987 it had become a cult programme like *Tiswas*, watched by many students and young adults. There were even *No 73* dances and balls!

There have been a number of other Saturday morning shows, the summer ones less high profile than those in winter. Summer Saturdays have a different feel. They are often interrupted by sport and it is more difficult to hold the audience. ITV made good use of its regional structure to set up formats like *Get Fresh* and *Ghost Train* (1989–91) which moved from area to area. They were co-ordinated by a central production team and made use of regional facilities. The BBC summer shows, including *The Saturday Picture Show* (1984–86) and *It's Wicked* (1987), tended to come from the north-west region. The most original was probably *On the Waterfront* (1988–89) which was made in a warehouse in Liverpool. It was more of a Light Entertainment show with sketches and games than a programme in the traditional magazine format.

In addition to the main Saturday morning magazines there have been a number of shows aimed at attracting the younger part of the audience early on. TV-am's *Wide Awake Club* presented by the exuberant Timmy Mallet is one example, as is the BBC's *Chucklevision* (1987–) and *Radio Roo* (1989–90), but the mainstay of the early morning schedule tends to be animation.

Although Saturday morning shows generally have smaller audiences than those during the week, they have a very high profile. They fill a lot of air-time and can attract top-rate guests. Leaders of all political parties have appeared on *Saturday Superstore* and *Going Live!* has featured guests including Sir Georg Solti, Dame Kiri Te Kanawa and Dudley Moore. The programmes are important shop windows for pop groups and personalities and provide platforms for the airing of issues. They also give access and opportunity. In 1991, *Going Live!* ran a competition to design the biggest mural in Europe, and the winning entry was painted on a blank end wall of TV Centre in White City, London.

There is a danger that, as money gets tighter and competition greater, these shows could degenerate into nothing more than presenters sitting on sofas linking pop promotion videos and cartoons, and interviewing people who have already been seen many times on the chat show circuit. Saturday morning television in the United States is made up of solid blocks of cartoons and the networks compete ruthlessly for ratings. Big companies like Disney, Warner Brothers and Hanna Barbera would be only too happy to dominate large blocks of United Kingdom air-time. *The Disney Club* (1989–), which mixes live activity with cartoons, is a ratings builder for ITV on Sunday mornings, and Warner Brothers provided major elements of the 1992 ITV autumn Saturday show *What's Up, Doc?* for STV. British Saturday morning television has created an identity for itself. It would be a pity to lose it.

CHAPTER SIX

Entertainment

All children's programmes need to be entertaining or they will not be watched, but there are a number of areas of programming which fall into an 'entertainment' category. They include factual entertainment, variety, sketch shows, game shows and quizzes, and situation comedy and comedy drama. Comedy is a notoriously difficult area, both for adults and children, and it is debatable whether children's comedy exists in its own right. Certainly, bad puns and lavatory jokes make children, but not their parents laugh, but they are not always easily translated into television. This is perhaps why there are fewer classics in this area of children's programming than in some others.

There are, of course, some outstanding and long-lived programmes. The most famous is probably *Crackerjack*. This began in 1955 and ran until 1984. It was originally made in the Children's Department of the BBC but moved to Light Entertainment in 1964 when the Children's Department was merged with Women's Programmes into Family Programmes. Johnny Downes was the first producer. In 1955 there was a problem about finding a studio for forthcoming children's programmes as the traditional one, Studio E in Lime Grove, was to be out of service. Johnny Downes suggested doing a programme for children from the Television Theatre on Shepherds Bush Green. It had been converted for use for television and continued to be used by the BBC, latterly for *Wogan*, until 1991. Freda Lingstrom, Head of the Children's Department, initially said 'no' to the idea, but changed her mind and suggested that Eamonn Andrews might be a good host.

Like all programmes at that time it was intended to have a limited run. Instead it became an institution. It was an ambitious show for its day. Originally forty-five minutes long, it was transmitted live at 5 p.m. with a rehearsal on the day itself. This put considerable strain on the three-man camera team and on the production team. Johnny Downes produced and directed, supported by a floor manager (the television equivalent of a stage

Crackerjack: Eamonn Andrews helping a winner to choose his prizes which always included the famous *Crackerjack* pencil. (BBC, 1961)

manager) and a secretary. In later days the size of the production team grew considerably.

Although the programme became more sophisticated over the years its basic format remained much the same. Certainly, the sketches became more elaborate and the advent of pop stars and pop videos had a considerable influence. But essentially *Crackerjack* was a mixture of a main presenter (Eamonn Andrews, Leslie Crowther, Michael Aspel, Ed Stewart, Stu Francis), comedy sketches, guest speciality acts and bands, and a game. The best known of the games was 'Double or Drop' where children received prizes for correct answers and cabbages for wrong ones. The consolation prizes for those who failed in the heats of the games were the famous *Crackerjack* pencils. Although 'Double or Drop' is the best-remembered game it did not continue throughout the life of the series. The format belonged to Eamonn Andrews and went when he did in 1964. It was bought back for BBC TV by producer Robin Nash in the 1970s.

There were a variety of other games. At one stage they were strictly divided into boys' games and girls' games. They now seem amazingly sexist with Eamonn Andrews making remarks like, 'And it was a girl who knew it, too!' in incredulous tones. The programme always had a grand finale involving the whole cast and over the years these became more elaborate. They seem very dated today, but the whole tradition of variety is also dated. The programmes undoubtedly had the right ingredients for their time and the level of humour, although sometimes toe-curling for adults, clearly worked for children. Despite a number of attempts, including *What's All This Then?* in 1987 and *The Satellite Show* (1988–89), the BBC has yet to create an entertainment programme which gives Friday afternoon the profile it had during the *Crackerjack* days. Maybe it is time to forget this kind of format and try to find a new one.

When Border Television revived the idea in 1988 for ITV in a similar show, *Crush a Grape*, hosted by Stu Francis, the last *Crackerjack* front man, it failed

Lift Off with Ayshea featuring Ayshea Brough. (Granada TV, 1969)

143

to attract the contemporary audience in really large numbers. Nevertheless, *Crackerjack* is one of those programmes which viewers remember with affection and nostalgia and has become very much a part of television history.

On the Waterfront (1988–89) from the BBC's Children's Unit in Manchester did perhaps have the makings of a new-style Light Entertainment programme, but it was broadcast on Saturday morning and because it did not work in this context it was not further developed.

Pop music played an increasingly important part in *Crackerjack* and for this reason, and because of *Top of the Pops*, which is not a children's programme but is watched by them in large numbers, the BBC has tended not to make specific pop programmes for children. *Cheggers Plays Pop* was an exception. However, pop is an integral part of Saturday morning and other programmes. ITV, on the other hand, has made a number of successful pop programmes over the years, many of them from Granada and produced by Muriel Young. They include *Lift Off with Ayshea* (1969–74) and *Shang-a-lang* (1975) with the Bay City Rollers. In the 1980s Tyne Tees specialized in pop with *Razzamatazz*, and produced the live teenage show *The Tube*. A BBC programme which explored the whole history of music from the Middle Ages onwards was *Price to Play*, introduced by Alan Price and produced by Peter Ridsdale-Scott.

Other classic programmes in the variety tradition featured puppets. Lenny the Lion, Basil Brush and Emu have had shows on both BBC and ITV. Basil Brush, the cheeky fox, was the idea of Peter Firmin, who created him for Ivan Owen, an ex-BBC assistant floor manager, to use on Associated Rediffusion's *The Three Scampis* in 1962. A few years later Owen produced him out of a bag for Johnny Downes who introduced him to David Nixon, and Basil Brush the star was born on BBC TV's *The Nixon Line*. He worked with David Nixon for several years until Nixon wanted to make commercials with him and the BBC bought him out. Basil then worked with a number of humans including Rodney Bewes, Derek Fowlds and Roy North. He will always be remembered for his manic laugh and his 'Boom! Boom!' punch-line. Unlike Basil Brush, the anarchic Emu has only ever worked with one human presenter, Rod Hull, plus innumerable fall guys. Emu is an aggressive and sometimes bad-tempered bird, and no respecter of persons. As far as children are concerned,

Play Away: (front row) Lionel Morton, Anne-Marie Hackett, Brian Cant and Toni Arthur, accompanied by the *Play Away* band (back row): Alan Rushton, Spike Heatley and Jonathan Cohen. (BBC, 1974)

the great attraction of Emu and, to a certain extent, Basil Brush is their ability to undermine the adult world in a way children would love to do themselves.

Play Away was one of the BBC's longest running music and sketch shows for children. It lasted from 1971 to 1984 and was a spin-off from *Play School*. *Play Away* was started because some extra money was coming in from the overseas sales of *Play School* and *Play School* kits. It was originally intended to be a fairly straightforward Saturday edition of *Play School*. However, it replaced the Saturday afternoon film on BBC 2 which dictated a much wider appeal to a family audience. Jokes were introduced very early on and the programme developed from there. Brian Cant remembers putting in an early joke while telling a story about making kites: 'What kind of paper makes a kite fly? Flypaper.'

Play Away gave the *Play School* presenters a chance to develop their talents. Brian Cant and Jonathan Cohen were the linchpins of the programme. Jonathan, the resident pianist and musical director, has his own place in the history of the BBC Children's Programmes. He had a traditional musical education and was playing in a folk festival when he was seen by a BBC Schools producer, John Hosier, who introduced him to Joy Whitby. Jonathan became an understudy pianist on *Play School* where he was trained by Bill Blezzard who, as well as being a *Play School* mainstay, was Joyce Grenfell's accompanist. Jonathan Cohen played an important part in the musical development of *Play Away*, and has provided music for innumerable children's programmes and series.

Play Away confirmed Brian Cant as one of the leading children's presenters of the day. He had not set out with a career in children's television in mind. He did not come from a theatrical background and had no formal training, but became interested in the theatre through the repertory theatre and music hall in Ipswich where he lived. He moved into repertory as a professional and worked for five years in various companies, particularly at Pitlochry in Scotland. He was working on a history programme for Schools Television – being a Roman figure on an urn – when he met Cynthia Felgate. She told him about the new programme she was about to work on,

Derek Griffiths
performing a rope trick
for *Play Away*.
(BBC, 1972)

Play School, and invited him to audition. From then on he made a real career in children's television and theatre, working for both the BBC and ITV.

Play Away was recorded as live and the music was also live, both in the studio and on location. This could cause problems at times. Although most of the programmes were made in the studio, there were a number of *Play Away* Away Days when the show was recorded on an outside location. One was even made aboard a narrow boat on a canal, with the piano and band on the boat. All the presenters remember the camaraderie of those days. At that time, in the 1970s, it was possible for a production of this kind to go out without props people or wardrobe and make-up. Everyone did everything for themselves.

Many *Play School* presenters graduated to *Play Away*, including Toni Arthur, Derek Griffiths and Johnny Ball. There were also some notable newcomers. Jeremy Irons made his television debut on the programme and Anita Dobson was auditioned at the same time as Patricia Hodge, who was turned down. A number of different programmes evolved out of *Play Away*. When the series ended, one of its principal producers, Ann Reay, went on to make a sketch series, *Fast Forward*, which developed the talents of Floella Benjamin and Nick Wilton among others.

The 'Think' series, presented by Johnny Ball, were also major developments out of *Play Away*. Johnny Ball had moved from the club circuit via *Play School* to *Play Away*. He had considerable comic talent but also an interest in science and numbers – and huge enthusiasm. The original idea was to make a fairly simple quiz and puzzle programme, but it evolved into a visual number and technology show presented in an entertaining way. *Think of a Number*, transmitted from 1977 to 1984, was successful both with its audience and in terms of winning major awards. *Think Again* (1981–85) concentrated on the technology behind everyday objects. Johnny Ball together with Albert Barber, the director and later producer of the shows, formed a strong partnership which created some truly innovative 'info-tainment' programmes. Johnny Ball later made a similar series of programmes for ITV, *Johnny Ball Reveals All* (1989–).

Record Breakers is another classic children's programme. It celebrated its twentieth birthday in 1991 hosted, as from the very beginning, by Roy Castle.

Think Again: Johnny Ball discovering facts about money with the help of a million pounds. (BBC, 1983)

Record Breakers: presenter Roy Castle with Chris Greener, the tallest man in Great Britain, and a model of the tallest ever man to live. (BBC, 1976)

It is based on the startingly simple concept which has also made *The Guinness Book of Records* a household name. As Roy Castle himself says, 'The appeal of the show remains the same. It's a wonderful mixture of some great people. Some are talented, some are completely mad, but all are genuine.' The programme has always collaborated closely with *The Guinness Book of Records* whose former editor, Norris McWhirter, appeared regularly on the programme. Between December 1972 and 1991 over 300 records were attempted on the programme and Roy Castle himself broke the tap dancing and parascending records. Alan Russell, who produced the show for many years, was responsible for many spectacular events including a mass tap dance in the courtyard of TV Centre.

ITV has made fewer sketch shows for children than the BBC. However, one of real note and historical interest is *Do Not Adjust Your Set* made by Associated Rediffusion, later Thames, between 1967 and 1969. The executive producer was Lewis Rudd and the programme producer was Humphrey

Barclay, a young Cambridge graduate who went on to become a distinguished producer of adult light entertainment shows. *Do Not Adjust Your Set* marked the first appearance of what was to become the Monty Python team. The artists were Terry Jones, Michael Palin, Eric Idle, David Jason, Denise Coffey and the Bonzo Dog Doo Dah Band. This is what the *Sunday Times* had to say about it on 28 January 1968:

> A funny thing happens on your TV screen on Thursday afternoon at 5.25 p.m. the tea-time spot – they're putting out another in the comedy series *Do Not Adjust Your Set*. It has no sexy sketches. No one comes on wearing drag. There are no jokes about politicians. It's adult in a way that those late night satirical shows never managed to be adult. But, in fact, it's a review designed specifically for children ... What's emerged is all first-hand stuff, very Goonish, with its own self-contained serial – a cold-eyed cod of all super-heroes called Captain Fantastic. Children love it. The only complaints come from adults who write in to say, 'I thought your programme was disgraceful and my two sons aged two and two and a half agreed.'

Do Not Adjust Your Set: Michael Palin, Eric Idle, Terry Jones (back row); David Jason and Denise Coffey (front row). (Associated Rediffusion, 1967)

Do Not Adjust Your Set was certainly a very innovative programme and, like all innovative programmes for children, it aroused parental ire. But it proves again that children's television often provides a platform for new talent. Lewis Rudd made this point at an IBA Children's Programmes Consultation in 1973, arguing that *Do Not Adjust Your Set* was the forerunner of *Monty Python's Flying Circus* and *The Goodies*, creating a major development in television comedy that would not have happened if it had not fitted in with the requirements of a children's programme schedule. He cited Southern's *Get This!* (1972–73), which also did not fit into any of the old pigeon-holes but had been allowed to happen, as another example of a children's programme that might well prove to have an appeal to a wider audience and become a pace-setter in its technique. This was certainly true: *Get This!* went on to be very successful. It is sad, however, that many other similar programmes have not risen to the standard of *Do Not Adjust Your Set*.

Quizzes and game shows have been a staple of all television from the early days. In children's television they were at first somewhat worthy and serious. Even in 'Double or Drop', the questions involved serious current affairs and nature study. There was a feeling that the BBC should not be too lighthearted. In 1962 the BBC transferred the highly successful *Top of the Form* from radio to television where it ran until 1975. Its more modern equivalent, from 1984 to 1988, was *Beat the Teacher* in which children competed with their teachers

Geoffrey Wheeler introduces another team taking part in *Top of the Form*. (BBC, 1963)

and were often able to beat them – an attractive proposition. This idea was taken up in a Saturday morning quiz, 'The Wetter the Better', part of *The 8.15 from Manchester*. It took place in a local sports complex and children could get their teachers dumped in the swimming-pool if they were able to outscore them. Clive Doig, who was behind *Beat the Teacher* (1984–88), also created other quizzes and 'info-tainment' shows for the BBC including *Puzzle Trail* (1980–84), *Noel Edmond's Lucky Numbers* (1978–79) and *Eureka!* (1982–86).

After the invention of 'gunge' in *Tiswas*, active, messy game shows became fashionable. Southern Television's *Runaround* (1976–81) was one such, and 'gunge' reached its peak in the BBC's 'Double Dare'. This was part of *Going Live!* and was a format bought in from the United States. Inventing game show formats has become big business and companies like Action Time, headed by Stephen Leahey, at one time Head of Granada's Children's Programmes, specialize in this. It is not easy to create new and attractive formats, particularly ones that have visual appeal and are not purely verbal. Basic game shows and quizzes are relatively cheap television. A number of editions can be recorded in a day – the more there are the lower the overall cost. The danger is that the content may be less than stimulating, and there is certainly a limit to the amount of scream and shout that is defensible and/or entertaining.

As technology has developed, so have game shows. BBC TV's *The Adventure Game*, transmitted between 1980 and 1986, was an innovative programme that used a combination of drama and computer graphics to lead the protagonists and the audience towards the solution of a series of problems. The programme often involved a maze. Anglia's *Knightmare* (1987–), which is aimed at eight to sixteen-year-olds, and Channel 4's *The Crystal Maze* (1990–), which is not strictly for children but much watched by them, both take the use of computer graphics far further and reflect the huge popularity of home computer games. The next development will be in Virtual Reality.

Comedy drama and situation comedy have been part of children's television since the 1950s. Both *Billy Bunter of Greyfriars School* and *Just William* made easy transitions from book to screen. *Billy Bunter* was transmitted between 1952 and 1961. The first producer, Joy Harington, was responsible for casting a thirty-year-old actor, Gerald Campion, as Bunter. Casting an adult in a child role would not be acceptable today. There were two series of *Just William*, in 1962 starring fourteen-year-old Dennis Waterman and in 1963 starring thirteen-year-old Denis Gilmore.

When the BBC children's drama output moved to the Drama Department there was a dearth of comedy for some time. *Here Come the Double Deckers*, screened in 1971, was a bought-in series from the United States. In 1973 there was the gentle humour of *Lizzie Dripping*, written by Helen Cresswell and starring Tina Heath who went on to become a *Blue Peter* presenter. There have been other dramas of this nature, aimed at the younger end of the audience. The BBC's *Simon and the Witch* (1987–88) and Central's *Woof* (1989–), which has an appealing canine star, are examples. The traditional, broader, comedy series were revived in 1976 with the advent of *Rentaghost* written by Bob Block, a veteran of adult situation comedy writing. It was produced first by Paul Ciani and then by Jeremy Swan who has specialized in

Woof, with James Ellis as Mr Fitzherbert and Tich as Eric the Dog. (Central TV, 1991)

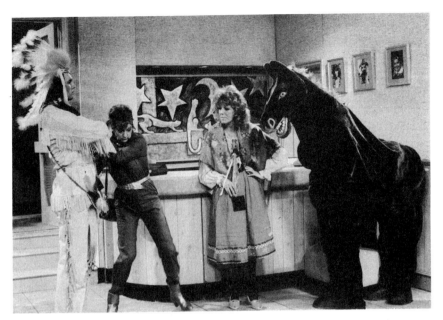

Rentaghost: (left to right) Maurice Thorogood (Big Chief Leaping Deer),
Ann Emery (Mrs Ethel Meaker) and Sue Nicholls (Nadia Popov) with Bill Terry
and John Asquith (Pantomime Horse). (BBC, 1982)

children's comedy over the years. Swan followed *Rentaghost* with *Grandad* (1979–84) starring Clive Dunn and *Galloping Galaxies* (1985–86). Later he produced *Bad Boyes* and, from 1990, *Uncle Jack* by Jim Eldridge. The latter starred Paul Jones and Fenella Fielding. *Rentaghost* and *Grandad* were both broad comedy. Neither featured children and both involved tricks and fantasy. *Rentaghost* was transmitted again in 1991 and pleased a completely new audience with its cast of bizarre ghosts and witches, the beleaguered Meaker family and the ever-present pantomime horse. Barbara Euphan Todd's famous scarecrow, Worzel Gummidge, made a brief appearance on BBC television in 1953, played by Frank Atkinson, but was far better known when played by Jon Pertwee for Southern Television in the late 1970s.

More special effects became available as television technology developed, and were used to good effect in series like Tyne Tees' *Supergran*, written by Jenny McDade and starring Gudrun Ure. Adult comedy is constantly developing and fashions change. The same is true in the children's area, particularly as more children are watching adult series. Yorkshire TV's *Round the Bend* which uses Spitting Image puppets and satirical humour is an example of changing fashions, as is the BBC's *Maid Marian and Her Merry Men*, the series written by Tony Robinson. Tony Robinson is a writer and performer with a wide range from dramatic story-telling, as in the BBC's *Odysseus* and *Boudicca*, to Baldrick in *Blackadder*. He has been a champion of quality children's television for many years, believing that its viewers should have the best and should be challenged and stimulated.

Maid Marian is broad comedy with many physical jokes, but it also works at a much more sophisticated level. The scripts are carefully crafted and the audience is taken seriously. The success of programmes like *Maid Marian*

Supergran starring Gudrun Ure on the Fly Cycle designed by Ashley Wilkinson. (Tyne Tees TV, 1985)

Maid Marian and Her Merry Men, written by and starring Tony Robinson (far left). (BBC, 1990)

and the Australian *Round the Twist*, broadcast in 1990, show that the child audience is ready to enjoy sophisticated comedy relevant to its own needs and interests. Equally, children are entertained by the simple and more basic comedy of *Rentaghost* and *Uncle Jack*.

It is clear that variety is needed and producers and writers must constantly be developing new ideas. Writing any comedy is hard. Writing comedy for children is really hard.

CHAPTER SEVEN

Conclusion

In its relatively short history, children's television has generated much heated debate – usually about its detrimental effect, as on the nation's Sunday School habits or on children's reading. It has been accused of increasing the incidence of violent behaviour in the young, encouraging bad language and copycat bad behaviour, and ruthless commercial exploitation.

There are two important factors to bear in mind when discussing these issues. The first is that television does not exist in isolation. It is part of a social framework which includes home, parents, school, teachers and friends. The second is that the subject under discussion is *children's* television. That is, television especially created for a child audience, not an adult one. Children have their own lives to lead and their own perspectives. Above all, they are not stupid. The greatest mistake adults make is to underestimate the child viewer. Children, even quite young ones, know the difference between stories and real life. When they are interviewed about their perception of *Grange Hill* they make it clear that they know the programme is fictional, that Grange Hill is not a real school, and that although the incidents in the programme are realistic they would not occur in the same patterns or structures in real life. There has to be an extraordinary level of dramatic incident in the programme to make it watchable, and the audience is quite capable of distinguishing fact from fiction.

When *Grange Hill* was first transmitted there was much outcry from parents who saw it as anti-authority and anarchic. But the whole philosophy of the series was to see school from a child's point of view. This extended even to the low camera angles that were used to help give the audience ownership of the programme. As one fourteen-year-old girl wrote in the *Radio Times* at the time of the controversy over the first series: 'I'm not saying that adults are not allowed to watch our programmes, but it was written for us, the children – the pupils at schools like *Grange Hill* who really understand what they are like.'

One development over the years is the greater enfranchisement of the audience. Originally, children's own voices were rarely heard and, if they were, they were mediated by adults. There was a theory that children would not listen to other children and were bored by seeing their peers. This thinking is no longer fashionable. Children are increasingly involved on the screen in a variety of roles, talking with confidence and authority. Another point that must be remembered is that today's child audience has grown up with television and understands the medium and the tricks of the trade.

Media studies appear on the curricula of many schools and children are increasingly able to experiment with their own videos. This generation knows how to manipulate the medium, and how the medium can manipulate the audience. However, the broadcasters who make and transmit children's programmes continue to have a real responsibility and, within the dedicated hours of children's time, remain *in loco parentis*. Their problem is to decide what kind of parent to be: careful and perhaps over-protective, or liberal and perhaps over-permissive. The broadcaster walks a tightrope and is constantly somewhere in the middle.

The BBC has guide-lines for children's programmes. They are guide-lines and not rules, and they are based on common sense. The old Independent Broadcasting Authority guide-lines were similar, as are those now published by the Broadcasting Standards Council. However, we have yet to see how the ITV companies will operate under the new lighter control from the Independent Television Commission combined with the guidance of the Broadcasting Standards Council. In any case, the satellite channels, which also broadcast for children, are not regulated in the same way. Hopefully, the tradition of responsibility and common sense which has evolved over the years will be maintained.

Bad language on television is a major cause of concern. In fact, no real bad language appears in children's programmes unless by mistake. Certainly, there is no acceptance of the kind of language that is common parlance in the playground. 'Flipping heck' is the strongest epithet that is used. Children who live in a real playground often find this attitude mealy-mouthed and feel it detracts from the credibility of the drama. It is worth noting that when *Swap Shop* invited the audience to send in jokes many were too rude for television. The use of words like 'God' or 'Christ' upsets many people but unfortunately, particularly on live television, these phrases sometimes slip out, especially from guests who are not trained in the mores of children's television. Again, it is not likely that the target audience will be shocked or harmed by these occasional slips.

Language in general arouses much feeling. Children's television is often accused of encouraging sloppy speech or paucity of vocabulary. In fact, it tries to reflect all kinds of speech and regional accents. Some adults have problems in understanding the Geordie accent in *Byker Grove*. Children don't appear to have any difficulty. It is important that children's television reflects all parts of the United Kingdom, not just London and the south-east, and that the widest range of regional accents can be heard.

The style used by presenters is another matter. Information needs to be conveyed at a reasonable pace, and intelligibly. There is a danger that

Andi Peters and Edd the Duck who preside over Children's BBC and the 'broom cupboard'. (BBC, 1992)

Children's ITV presenter Tommy Boyd. (1992)

shouting and over-exuberance is sometimes confused with 'street cred' and identifying with the audience. It is hard to define what makes a good children's presenter. It is clearly not just a question of age. Tony Hart and Roy Castle are as successful now as they were in their youth. Personality is obviously important. The presenter must have warmth and be able to communicate via the screen and subdue his or her own ego. Authority is important but not essential. John Noakes was no less loved because of his frequent lapses of memory. In fact, that was one of the characteristics that endeared him to the audience. Presenters should not be silly, although they should have the ability to make fun of themselves. Above all, they should not patronize. Talking down is the cardinal sin of children's presenters.

Presenters come from a variety of backgrounds. Tony Hart became one by chance. On the other hand, it was the only thing Tommy Boyd, of *Magpie*, now a presenter of links for Children's ITV, ever wanted to be. Phillip Schofield, who really wanted to be in radio not television, started in New

Zealand and made his name in BBC TV's 'broom cupboard'. Sarah Greene and Tina Heath were actresses. Valerie Singleton (*Blue Peter*) and Bunty James (*How*) started as continuity announcers. But, however people start, they all agree it is not an easy job. It requires a variety of skills from a good memory to athletic prowess, courage and a sense of humour.

Children's presenters have a special responsibility in that they are perceived as role models and have the power to influence. Tommy Boyd says his philosophy is that you can show children it is possible to get on in life by being nice, articulate and intelligent rather than just glitzy and showbiz. Phillip Schofield says he is himself a non-hysterical type. Sarah Greene says she thinks of herself as a person, not a role model, and the audience as real people to whom she is talking. This underlines the necessity of taking the audience seriously.

Violence is the other major concern within children's television. In 1987 a committee chaired by Will Wyatt, then Head of Documentary Features, Television, examined the whole issue of violence. As regards children they made a number of points including the following:

> The impression should not be given that violence does not lead to injury. Frightening scenes should be considered with great care and thought given to how children of all ages might cope.

> Do not linger on death scenes or frightening close-ups.

> Avoid dangerous situations which could be easy for children to imitate, e.g. karate chops, weapons which are easily accessible, knives, ropes, broken bottles, etc., scenes in which people are locked up in empty rooms or cellars, or hide in old refrigerators or ovens.

> Good characters and those with whom children identify should where possible only use legitimate and legal means to achieve their objectives.

These points are reiterated in the current producers' guide-lines. Section 12(c) on violence in children's programmes reads as follows:

> There is evidence that violence in circumstances resembling real life is more upsetting than violence in a fantasy setting. The distress felt by

some adults when violence occurs in familiar settings or between familiar figures is likely to be increased in the case of children. Violence in situations (for instance in the home between characters resembling their parents) or towards characters (for example pets) with which the child can sympathize should therefore be avoided.

Although it is morally satisfying, especially to children, to witness the success of good over evil, the means employed by good characters should be carefully chosen in order to avoid confusion with the bad characters.

The dangers of imitation are particularly real among children for whom it is important not to conceal consequences of real life violence. For example, a blow to the head must not in a realistic setting be seen as a trivial matter without serious consequences.

These recommendations are clearly sensible, but there will be times when some violence is required to tell the story. In Bernard Ashley's *Running Scared*, for example, transmitted by the BBC in 1986, there was a violent robbery which set up the whole plot, and it was necessary to make the sequence convincing and frightening. In a case like this, it is a question of the degree of violence and the way in which it is shown on the screen. There was a sequence in *Grange Hill* which showed a bottle fight in a pub. In the original transmission, there was a shot of the bottle making impact on a person's head. On reflection, it was decided that this was too violent and it was removed for the repeat showing. However, the sequence immediately afterwards, which showed one of the boys being sick, was left in despite adverse comments. It was felt that it showed very graphically the effect the fight had had on the protagonists. If violence is used in such dramatic sequences, it is important that the consequences are also shown.

The research that has been done on the causal relationship between television and violence is inconclusive, and it is clear that many other factors are involved. In any case, the real problem about children and violence and bad language probably arises outside the dedicated children's hours and comes when children watch adult television up to and beyond the 9 p.m. watershed. Maire Messenger Davies puts these issues firmly into context:

In the light of the bad press that television's influence on children consistently receives, it needs to be said again that the childhood attraction to mischief and even downright brutality is not a recent development. It has always been there and appears to be intrinsic to certain periods of childhood and to certain types of child. Not portraying it in stories or on television will thus not do away with it. Developmental studies have shown that there seem to be peak ages for aggression – at around two to three years old and later in the early teens. Other periods of childhood are relatively calm. There are obvious and long-standing sex differences in aggression too. Boys on the whole are more likely to be aggressive than girls, and men are much more likely to be violent than women. Both sexes watch television, indeed women watch more, so television cannot be held to account for this gender difference in anti-social behaviour. As long as television is almost exclusively blamed for violence in society, the real origins of these differences can conveniently be left unexplored . . .

Television is unlikely to be able to override the influence of family in the community. Its influence will be strongest when it is going in the direction in which the child or adult viewer already wants to go. This is what advertisers rely on, this is what will make a programme more commercially influential.

Another major area of controversy in children's television is that of merchandising. There has always been merchandise. Sooty was merchandised, as was Muffin the Mule. BBC Publications produced *Play School* and *Jackanory* books from the start of the programmes, and there were records and audio-tapes and, in later years, videos. However, toys have been the major problem; in particular toys linked with American animation series. The first time this really arose was in 1981, when the BBC bought *Thundercats*. The second time was over the *Teenage Mutant Hero (Ninja) Turtles* series. Both were big successes and so was the merchandising. The *Turtles* did exceptionally well because of the release of the feature film.

The main issue is not that toys exist, but whether or not a series is editorially driven by the toy manufacturers so that a programme becomes nothing more than a half-hour commercial for specific products. In both cases mentioned above, the BBC bought the series on the strength of the programmes and the knowledge that they would be successful with the audience. In neither case was the series directly financed by toy manufacturers, although a second series of *Turtles*, which was not purchased, was. Quality of programming is the first criterion. The second is editorial control.

At a European Broadcasting Union seminar in York in 1991, series producer Verena Billeter discussed the highly successful *Pingu* programmes, an animation about penguins for small children, which the BBC had bought. Because it was so successful, there had been much pressure from toy manufacturers who wanted to dictate the story-line and introduce new characters – pressure which, so far, had been resisted by the programme-makers. It is a complicated, chicken-and-egg situation. Animation costs money; television producers do not have enough money; merchandising makes money. Some of the profits can be reinvested in new animation. This is the principle on which the BBC Children's Department works with BBC Enterprises, but it is absolutely clear that the Children's Department has editorial control, right of veto over projects and approval of licences and merchandising.

There is absolutely nothing wrong with television programmes having an extended life in other media. Grown-ups may have hated turtle toys and turtle T-shirts – children loved them as they have loved Cindy, My Little Pony and Paddington Bear. Parents always have the right to say no, or to encourage their offspring to make the do-it-yourself versions *Blue Peter* deliberately features. It may well be that in ten years time the heart-searching about who finances what may seen unnecessarily tortuous. What will remain crucial is who takes the editorial decisions.

Is children's television an endangered species? Is it worth preserving? Is it special anyway? I believe the answer to all these questions is: yes.

If you look at public service television channels around the world, including many that, like ITV, are founded by advertising, the picture tends to be gloomy. In the United States, despite the best efforts of Peggy Charren and Action for Children's Television, whose president she was, there is little real children's television and it is confined to public broadcasting and specialized cable channels. Wonderworks, one of the outstanding groups, which operated on behalf of a group of public service broadcasting stations and specialized in high-quality drama, often co-produced with United Kingdom companies, will cease to exist in 1992, the funding being transferred to a new Children's Television Workshop production. Doubtless this will be of high quality, but there should be room and finance for both. Nickelodeon, the cable channel owned by Music Television (MTV), a satellite cable station that shows pop videos, does excellent work. However, the programmes it transmits are a drop in the ocean compared with hours of terrestrial mainstream programming filled with good, average and sometimes awful animation.

Australia and Canada are not much better. In Canada, the Canadian Broadcasting Corporation has an ambiguous attitude to children's programmes – sometimes supportive, sometimes not. CBC has very little in-house children's production. Major strands are commissioned from independent producers. This has resulted in some excellent productions like *Degrassi Junior High* and *Anne of Green Gables*, but there is no longer the body of bread-and-butter, home-produced programmes which, at one stage,

Degrassi Junior High with Amanda Cook as L.D. (CBC, 1988)

The Animals of Farthing Wood, a new animation series based on the novels of Colin Dann. Nineteen major public service broadcasters, all members of the EBU, came together to fund this series which was made half in the UK by Telemagination and half in France by La Fabrique. (BBC, 1993)

rivalled the variety provided by the BBC and ITV, although there are signs that things may change in the future. TV Ontario continues to make pre-school programmes, and some original programmes are made by Radio Canada in Quebec, but Canadian television is dominated by series from over the border.

In Australia, the Australian Broadcasting Corporation continues to make Australian *Play School*, but the Children's Department is much reduced and is primarily concerned with commissioning. The present head of the department is an administrator with no track record in children's programming. One of the strongest influences in Australian children's television is the Australian Film and Television Foundation led by Patricia Edgar. She has fought long and hard to create real quality programming for children. She managed, after much lobbying, to raise funds to make the drama series *Winners*, and later the comedy drama series *Round the Twist* which the BBC transmitted in 1990 with some success. Her latest project is *Lift Off*, an ambitious, early learning series.

Another banner-carrier in Australia is Penny Spence, a children's producer who has worked for various commerical channels, who persuaded the channel she then worked for to participate in the EBU exchanges, and made a number of distinguished programmes including the prize-winning dramas *Danny's Egg* and *The Water Trolley*. Other producers are struggling to maintain quality and standards, but they work in an increasingly competitive world where television programmes are 'product' in the way that baked beans are, and ratings are desperately important. They are not helped by Australia's well-meant, but unnecessarily restrictive, Children's Committee which certificates children's programming. In 1991, the role of this committee changed and it is now concerned with the validation of production companies.

In Europe, as competition from satellite television builds up, public service television channels in countries like Germany and France see their audience falling to the alternative schedules of international game shows and animation series. However, there are some rays of hope. In Italy, the child audience has begun to return to home-produced programmes on Radio Televisone Italiana. In Scandinavia, the children still seem to be loyal to traditional fare.

It is clear that unless there is a real commitment to children's programmes, not just from the specialists but also from the directors of programmes and management boards, they will wither and die in terms of mainstream terrestrial transmission. It could be argued that, provided the service is available somewhere on cable or satellite, being part of mainstream broadcasting is not that important. But it is unlikely that anyone would be prepared to invest the amount of money required to maintain the current range and variety of programming – a commercial return is by no means guaranteed.

Children's television of the type that Britain has had in the past is never going to be hugely profitable. But the appetitie for it continues, and it is important that the new generation of children should have the opportunities their parents had.

What is so special about children's television as it has developed in Britain? Firstly, it is geared to its audience. It studies children's needs, researches its impact and takes the viewer seriously. Throughout the world it is apparent that the people who work in children's television do not do so for money or glory or power. They are in it because they believe it is important, and they enjoy their work. The response programme-makers get from children is direct and fulfilling: 60 000 shouting children at the naming of the *Blue Peter* engine in 1970, the 'Tingha and Tucker children' at Woburn. Children do not just watch their television, they live it as well, entering competitions, making models, writing stories, for example. They give something back to the programme-makers in a way that does not happen in adult television. Children's television is a two-way activity.

Another thing which has been important is the way in which people have dedicated their professional lives to children's television. As has been seen in previous chapters, the same names recur: Lewis Rudd, Muriel Young, Dorothea Brooking, Molly Cox, Cynthia Felgate, Ann Reay, Anne Gobey and myself. We operate in a relatively small world and, because of our mutual concern for the audience and the standards of the output, we have always talked to, and supported, each other. In this way, a continuity has been created in British children's television, and with it the development of a programme-making philosophy which may well now be unique. This kind of continuity was possible all the time there were in-house children's departments but it may no longer be so with the advent of large numbers of independent producers and an increase in companies that commission all their programmes from outside sources. Hopefully, new areas of expertise will develop and traditions will be handed on as they were in the past. Hopefully, also, new generations of children will get the television service they deserve and should have. Television should never be taken too seriously, but children's television should be taken more seriously than most.

Major Milestones of Children's Programmes

Compiled by P.R. Jackson

1946   First children's programme – *For The Children* (BBC) transmitted. Several months later Muffin the Mule made his first appearance with Annette Mills.

1950   BBC Children's Department formed.

Mrs Clement Attlee opened the new Lime Grove Studios which became the home for children's programmes.

Andy Pandy (BBC) came out to play for the first time.

Peter Hawkins, 'the voice' of later children's favourites, first appeared on *Whirligig* (BBC).

1952   Character of Billy Bunter played by Gerald Campion first appeared in *Billy Bunter of Greyfriars School* (BBC).

Tony Hart first appeared on *Saturday Special* (BBC) – start of a forty-year association with BBC TV.

First programme for children with impaired hearing – *For Deaf Children* (BBC).

Character of Sooty first appeared in children's programmes with Harry Corbett on *Saturday Special* (BBC).

Bill and Ben *The Flowerpot Men* (BBC) came out of their garden pots for the first time.

1954   First production by BBC Television Puppet Theatre – later produced *Toytown* and *Rubovia* programmes.

1955   *The Woodentops* (BBC) along with Spotty Dog first appeared.

Crackerjack (BBC) first transmitted with a chance of winning the famous Crackerjack pencil.

ITV began broadcasting.

Johnny Morris first appeared as *The Hot Chestnut Man* (BBC).

The Adventures of Robin Hood (ATV) starring Richard Greene first transmitted.

1956   *Zoo Time* (Granada) first transmitted.

Character of Lenny The Lion (BBC) first appeared with Terry Hall.

1957   Toddlers' Truce from 6–7pm on BBC TV ended – ITV filled the hour with filmed adventure series.

Character of Captain Pugwash (BBC) and his crew on the *Black Pig* took to the sea for the first time.

Characters of Pinky and Perky (BBC) first appeared.

1958   *Blue Peter* (BBC) set sail for the first time as a weekly magazine series.

1962   Characters of Tingha and Tucker (ATV) appeared with former ATV announcer Jean Morton for the first time.

Animal Magic (BBC) with Keeper Johnny Morris first transmitted.

Character of Basil Brush first appeared in *The Three Scampis* (A/R); later appeared with David Nixon and in his own series.

1963   BBC Children's Department disbanded with drama and light entertainment going to the adult departments.

Tony Hart designed the familiar *Blue Peter* ship logo used on the opening titles, famous badges and stationery/merchandising.

1964   BBC Family Programmes Department took over the children's programmes output.

Vision On (BBC) first transmitted with the first pictures appearing in 'The Gallery'.

Play School (BBC) with its familiar house, windows and toys appeared for the first time – also the first programme to be shown on BBC 2.

1965   *Thunderbirds* (ATV) went to the rescue for the first time.

The Magic Roundabout (BBC) first transmitted.

Jackanory (BBC) began story-telling.

1966   *How* (Southern) first transmitted.

1967   BBC Children's Department reformed again.

1968   *Junior Showtime* (Yorkshire) first transmitted.

Magpie (Thames) first transmitted.

Characters of Sooty and Pinky and Perky made their first appearances on ITV after being axed by the BBC in 1967.

1972   First regular news programme for children – *John Craven's Newsround* (BBC) – began.

Rainbow (Thames) first transmitted.

Record Breakers (BBC) began setting their own records.

1974   *Tiswas* (ATV/Central) began disrupting Saturdays.

1976   *The Muppets* (ATV) first transmitted.

Multi-Coloured Swap Shop (BBC) opened up the phone lines and started swapping for the first time.

1977   Character of Morph appeared for the first time in *Take Hart* (BBC).

1978   School term began at *Grange Hill* (BBC).

1982   Channel 4 began broadcasting.

1983   Introduction of Children's ITV with a new umbrella logo for all ITV regions.

TV-am (ITV's breakfast station) began broadcasting – later rescued by the puppet character Roland Rat.

1985   Introduction of Children's BBC and the 'broom cupboard' presided over by Phillip Schofield.

Index

Action for Children's Television 163
Action Time 151
Adams, Mary 15–17
Adventure Game, The 151
Adventures of Black Beauty, The (Anna Sewell) 96, *96*
Adventures of Robin Hood, The 35, 95, *95*
Adventures of Twizzle, The 61
Ahlberg, Allan & Janet 107
Aiken, Joan 83, 96
Ain't Many Angels 106
Alexandra Palace 15, 21, 23
All About Animals 117
All Star Record Breakers 105
All Your Own 25, *25*, 32
Anderson, Gerry 47, 61, 130
Andrews, Eamonn 141–3, *142*
Andy Pandy 30, 32, 49–52, *51*
Anglia Television 36, 120, 151
Animal Magic 40, *116*, 117–18
Animals in Action 120
Animals of Farthing Wood, The 68, 165
Anne of Green Gables 164
Anneka 103
Annis, Francesca 47
Appleyards, The 32, *33*, 101
Ardizzone, Edward 82
Arnold, Andrea 120, *136*
Art Attack 123
Arthur, Toni 147
Ashcroft, Chloe 71, *73*
Ashley, Bernard 92, 101, 161
Associated Rediffusion (AR) 19, 40, 47, 61–2, 86, 94, 95, 144, 148
Attenborough, (Sir) David 34, *34*, 117
Atterbury, Audrey 51
ATV (Associated Television) 47–8, 56, 57, 61, 130, 134
Australian Broadcasting Corporation (ABC) 165
Australian Children's Film and Television Foundation 45
Australian Film and Television Foundation 165

Babar the Elephant 17, 67
Bagpuss 62, *63*

Baldwin, Nigel 105
Ball, Johnny 73, 117, 147, *148*
Ballet Shoes 9, 27
Barber, Albert 71, 147
Barclay, Humphrey 148, 149
Barnes, Edward 110, 112, 117, 125
Basil Brush 40, 58, *58*, 144–5
Baverstock, Donald 36
Baxter, Biddy 110, 112–14
BBC (British Broadcasting Corporation) 9, 12–15, 18–19, 23, 25–9, 34–7, 39–46, 48–9, 52, 54–5, 60–2, 65–8, 70–1, 74–80, 85–8, 90–4, 96–8, 100–2, 104–5, 107–8, 114–21, 123–6, 128, 130–1, 134–5, 138–48, 150–4, 157, 160, 162–3
BBC General Advisory Council 38
Beat That 124
Beat the Teacher 150–1
Beeching, Angela 85
Beetle Called Derek, A 120
Bell, David 86
Bellamy's Bugle 121
Belle and Sebastian 40
Bellinger, Chris 133
Bengo 79
Benjamin, Floella 147
Bertha 65
Bewes, Rodney 58, *58*, 144
Beynon, Mike 118, 119
Big Six, The 97
Biggles 27
Bill and Ben (see also *Flowerpot Men, The*) 25, 49, 50–1
Billeter, Verena 163
Billy Boy 105
Billy Bunter of Greyfriars School 22, 32, 87, *88*, 102, 151
Bird, Maria 30, 51
Birkbeck, Paul 75, 85, 117
Black Arrow, The 27, 28, 88
Blackadder 86, 154
Blaikley, Alan 106
Blake, Quentin *81*, 83
Bleasdale, Alan 135
Blezzard, Bill 146
Block, Bob 152
Blood and Honey 86
Blue Peter 9, 13, 22, 36, 37, 40–1, 47, 79, 98, 109–17, *110*, 112–15, 117,

121, 123, 125, 130–1, 152, 160, 163, 167
Bond, Michael 64
Book Tower, The 124
Bookshop on the Quay 90
Border Television 143
Boswell, Ruth 99
Boudicca 154
Box of Delights, The 87, 94
Boyd, Tommy 159, *159*, 160
Brendan Chase 96
Bric-A-Brac 71
British Action for Children's Television (BACTV) 12
Broadcasting Standards Council 128, 157
Bronze, Lewis 113
Brooking, Dorothea 18, *18*, 21, 70, 91–2, 113, 167
Brown, Pamela 18, 19
Buchanan, Neil 123
Butterworth, Peter 29, 34
Button Moon 85
Byker Grove 14, 88, 158

Cabbages and Kings 71
Cabin in the Clearing 88
Camberwick Green 65
Campion, Gerald *88*, 151
Canadian Broadcasting Corporation (CBC) 108, 164
Cansdale, George 117
Cant, Brian 71, 77, 145–6
Cant, Colin 102
Capon, Naomi 18
Captain Planet 117
Captain Pugwash 67
Caravan Children 27
Carpenter, Richard 95
Carrie's War 92, *93*
Cartoon Forum 68
Carty, Todd 102, *104*
Casey Jones 40
Castle, Roy 147–8, *148*, 159
Catweazle 95
CBTV 115
Central Television 14, 64, 96, 102–3, 105, 106, 116, 152
Champion The Wonder Horse 35
Changes, The 100, 101

Channel 3 11–12
Channel 4 45, 66, 107, 123–4, 151
Charlton, Peter 71
Charren, Peggy 163
Cheggers Plays Pop 144
Chegwin, Keith 131, *132, 138*
Chell, Carol 71
Childline 127
Children of Green Knowe, The 89, 90
Children's Film Unit 107, *108*
Children's Film and Television
    Foundation 107
Children's Hour (BBC Radio) 13, 15,
    79, 87
Children's Hour (BBC TV) 15, 21, 22
Children's ITV 159
Children's Newsreel 17, 74, 124, 126
Children's Television Workshop
    (CTW) 42–5, 117, 123, 164
Children's Ward 13, 14, 102, *102*, 103,
    116
Chock-A-Block 71
Chronicles of Narnia, The 92, 93, 94
Chucklevision 140
Ciani, Paul 105, 152
Clangers, The 62
Claridge, David 60
Clocks and Blocks 52
Clutterbuck, Graham 64–5
Codename Icarus 92
Coffey, Denise 149, *149*
Cohen, Jonathan 145, 146
Cole, Michael 71, *73*
Conker King, The 31
Cookson, Catherine 90–1
Cooney, Joan Ganz 42
Cooper, Richard 92
Coot Club 97
Corbett, Harry 20, 54–5, *55*
Corbett, Matthew 55, *56*, 76
Corners 71, 78, 115
Coronet Capers 105
Cosgrove Hall 62, 64
Count Duckula 64
Country Boy 47
Country Search 115
Covington, Julie 105
Cowell, Eileen 82
Cox, Molly 70, 80, 85, 117, 167
Crackerjack 40, 141–2, *142*, 143–4
Crane 47
Crane, Andy 56
Craven, John 125–6, *126*, 128
Cresswell, Helen 92, 96–8, 152
Cribbins, Bernard 82, 105
Crystal Maze, The 151
Cruise of the Toytown Belle 27

Crush A Grape 143
Crystal Tipps and Alistair 65

Dahl, Roald 84, 107
Dale, John 136
Danger – Marmalade at Work 84
Dangermouse 64
Dann, Colin 68
Danny, The Champion of the World
    107
Danny's Eggs 166
Danot, Serge 65–6
Davies, Andrew 84
Davies, Maire Messenger 85, 161
Davies, Marion *114*, 115
Davies, Nicola 119
Degrassi Junior High 108, 164, *164*
Dench, (Dame) Judi 82–3
Deputy Dawg 39
Dickinson, Peter 92, 100
Dimbleby, Richard 12, *26*
Dinenage, Fred *114*, 115
Disney 45, 47, 64, 67, 137, 140
Dizzy Heights 60
Do Not Adjust Your Set 40, 148–9, *149*,
    150
Dr Who 41, 101
Docurama 116
Dog So Small, A 83
Doig, Clive 151
'Double Dare' (*Going Live!*) 151
'Double or Drop' (*Crackerjack*) 142,
    150
Dowling, Patrick 122
Downes, Johnny 141, 144
Driscoll, Patricia 80, *95*
Duggan, Wendy 74
Duncan Dares 115
Duncan, Peter 113, 115
Dunn, Clive 152–3
Dyke, Greg 60

Eason, Ursula 36, *37*, 55, 121–2
Ed and Zed 130
Edd the Duck 56, 111
Edgar, Patricia 165
Edmonds, Noel 131, *132*
8.15 from Manchester, The 151
Eldridge, Jim 153
Elizabeth II, HM Queen 32
Ellis, Janet 109, 112
Emperor's Nightingale, The 53
Emu 144–5
Essex, Francis 45
Eureka! 151
European Broadcasting Union (EBU)
    105, 163, 166

Ewoks 67

Fabulous Animals 117
Fallon, Michael 9, 85
Famous Five, The 48
Fast Forward 147
Felgate, Cynthia 69, 71, 76, 77, 78, 85, 146,
    167
Fielding, Yvette 112
Filmfair 64
Fingermouse 78
Fireball XL5 61
Fireman Sam 65
Firmin, Peter 62, *63*, 144
Five Children and It 27, *27*, 28
Five O'Clock Club 47
Flashing Blade, The 40
Flockton Flyer, The 48, 96
Flowerpot Men, The 13, 25, 30, *52*
Floyd, Gareth 83
Follyfoot 96, *96*
For Deaf Children 122
For The Children 15–16
Foreman, Michael 65
Four Feather Falls 61
Fowlds, Derek 58, 144
Fox, Marilyn 91, 94, 101
Fox, (Sir) Paul 55, 125
Fraggle Rock 58
Francis, Stu 142–3
Fun Factory 135

Galloping Galaxies 153
Garfield, Leon 67
Garscadden, Kathleen (Auntie
    Cyclone/Kathleen) 15
Gay, Jennifer 26, *26*
George's Marvellous Medicine 84
Get Fresh 139
Get This! 150
Ghost Train 139
Gill, Rosemary 110, 130–1
Go with Noakes 115
Gobey, Anne 71, 167
Going Live! 119, 121, 123, 129, 132,
    133–4, 137–8, *139*, 140, 151
Going Out 104
Goodies, The 150
Grace, Chris 67
Grade, (Lord) Lew 57, 61
Grade, Michael 49
Graham's Gang 41
Granada Television 13–14, 47, 61, 96,
    102–3, 107, 116, 135, 144, 151
Grandad 152, 153
Grange Hill 13–14, 41, 71, 88, 101–2,
    104, 106, 116, 123, 127, 156–7, 161

Great Big Groovy Horse 105
Great Expectations 88
Greene, Sarah 107, 133, *139*, 160
Grenfell, Joyce 82, 146
Griffiths, Derek *73*, *146*, 147
Groom, Simon *110*, 113

Haley, (Sir) William 17
Hanna Barbera 67, 140
Hargreaves, Jack 47, *114*, 115
Harington, Joy 18, 87, *89*, 151
Harlech Television 106
Harris, Peter 134
Harris, Rolf 20
Hart, Tony 33, 47, *121*, 122–3, 159
Hartbeat 33, 122
Haunting of Cassie Palmer, The 91
Hawkins, Peter 25, 33, 47, 51
Hayes, Geoffrey 76
Hayles, Brian 98
Hayton, Hilary 65, 75
He Man 67
Heath, Tina 113, 152, 160
Henry, Lenny 134
Henson, Jim 42, 58–9, *59*, 61
Here Come the Double Deckers 152
Hodge, Patricia 105, 147
Hodson, Phillip 133
Hogarth Puppets 16
Holman, Roger 105
Home, Anna 49, 70, 78, 80, 90–1, 100, 102, 167
Home and Away 108
Hood, Stuart 36
Hopalong Cassidy 35
Hot Chestnut Man, The 79, *79*
How 48, *114*, 115, 160
How 2 48
Howard, Ken 106
Huckleberry Finn 34, 87
Hughes, Ted 83
Hull, Rod 144
Hunter Blair, John 109
Husson, Geoff 105, 124

IBA (Independent Broadcasting Authority) 12, 45–7, 150, 157
Idle, Eric 149, *149*
In The Beginning 85
Ipso Facto 101, 116
Iron Man, The 83
Island of the Great Yellow Ox 91
ITC (Independent Television Commission) 12, 157
It's Wicked 139
ITV (Independent Television) 9, 11, 12, 26, 34–5, 39, 42, 45, 47–8, 55–6, 60–2, 65, 67, 75, 78, 84–6, 92, 95–6, 104–5, 113, 115, 116, 120–1, 124, 129–30, 134, 136, 139–40, 143–4, 147–8, 157, 163

Jackanory 22, 37, 40, 46, 75, 80, *81*, 82–6, 89, 162
Jackanory Playhouse 104
James, Bunty 115, 160
James, Sally 134, *135*
Jason, David 149, *149*
Jenkin, May (Auntie Elizabeth) 15
Jennings 102
Jesus of Nazareth 87–8
Joe and the Gladiator 90–1, *92*
John Craven's Newsround 17, 41, 125, *126*, 128
Johnny Ball Reveals All 147
Jones, Daphne 70, 75
Jones, Paul 105, 153
Jones, Terry 149, *149*
Jonny Briggs 84, 107
Jordan, Diane-Louise *110*, 113
Joshua Jones 65
Josie Smith 107
Journey to the Centre of the Earth 39
Junior Criss-Cross Quiz 47
Junior Inventors Club, The 27
Junior Points of View 40
Junior Sports Week 47
Just A Normal Girl 124
Just William 151–2

Katy 88
Ken Dodd and the Diddymen 41
Keysell, Pat *121*, 122
King of the Golden River, The 53
Kirby, Alex 94
Knight For A Day 52
Knightmare 151
Knights of God 93

La Fabrique 68
Larry the Lamb (*Toytown*) 16, 49
Lassie 35
Last Man Out, The 88
Laurel and Hardy 41
Lay On Five 78
Learning Corporation of America 105
Leigh, Roberta 61
Lenny the Lion 144
Leslie, John *110*, 112
Lestocq, Humphrey 20, *20*, 29
Lettie 124
Letts, Barry 89
Lewis, Cecil (Uncle Caractacus) 15
Lift Off 165

Lift Off with Ayshea 143, 144
Likely Lad, A 93
Lime Grove Studios 21–2, 51, 141
Lingard, Joan 104
Lingstrom, Freda 19, *19*, 27, 29, 30–2, 34, 42, 51, 55, 141
Lion, The Witch and the Wardrobe, The 94
Listen With Mother (BBC Radio) 68, 77
Little Fire Engine, The 27
Little Grey Rabbit 27, 83
Little Women 87, 88
Lizzie Dripping 96, 98, 152
London Weekend Television (LWT) 37, 45–6, 95–6
Long Way Home, A 88
Lonsdale, Pamela 94
Look At Me 105
Lowdown, The 116

McCallum, Graham 75, 85
McCulloch, Derek (Uncle Mac) 15
McDade, Jenny 153
McGivern, Cecil 16, 18, 28, 30, 32, 34
McKechnie, Vera 79–80
McWhirter, Norris 148
Madden, Cecil 19–20, *20*, 28–9
Maggie 104
Magic Roundabout, The 9, 37, 40, 65–7, *66*
Magpie 40, 46, 47, 113–15, 159
Maid Marian and her Merry Men 154, *155*
Mallet, Timmy 140
Man Dog 100
Marine Boy 39
Martinez, Mina 75
Men at Work 30–31
Meridian 12
Mersey Pirate, The 134
Michelmore, Cliff 20, 25, 32–3
Mickey Mouse 15
Midnight Is A Place 96
Miller, Jon *114*, 115
Miller, Peggy 41
Mills, Annette 16, 50
Mrs Pepperpot 83
Monty Python team 149
Moon Stallion, The 41, 98
Moondial 96–8
Morris, Desmond 47
Morris, Johnny 79, *79*, *116*, 118
Morris, Juliet 129
Morton, Jean 47, 56, 57, *57*
Motormouth 120, 121, 137–8
Motormouth 2 137
Moult, Ted *72*, 74

Muffin the Mule 13, 16, 28, 41, 50–1, 50, 55, 162
Multi-Coloured Swap Shop 41, 130, 132
Muppets, The 42, 44–5, 58, 59
Murray, Gordon 16, 52–3, *54*
Music Television (MTV) 164
My Brother David 116
My Naughty Little Sister 83

Nash, Robin 142
Neighbours 13, 108
Nelvana 67
New Beginning, The 85
Newsround 13, 126–9
Newsround Extra 129
Nicholas Nickleby 105
Nickelodeon 64, 164
Nimmo, Derek 52
Nixon Line, The 144
Noakes, John *110*, 112, 115, 159
Noddy 27
Noel Edmond's Lucky Numbers 151
North, Roy 144
Now Then 117
No 73 120, 135–6, *136*, 138–9
Nutkins, Terry 119
Nutley, Colin 103

Odysseus 154
Odyssey, The 86
Oliver Twist 36
On Safari 117
On the Waterfront 139, 144
Orion 106
Orlando (Kathleen Hale) 17
Orlando (AR drama series) 47
Our John Willie 91
Owen, Ivan 58, 144
Owl Service, The 96
Owl TV 117

Packham, Chris 119, *119*
Paddington 64
Palin, Michael 149, *149*
Paradise Walk 88, 101
Parallel 9 138
Parnell, Margaret 111
Peacock, Michael 36, 68, 80
Penny Crayon 34
Pertwee, Jon 153
Philbin, Maggie 131
Pickard, Nigel 136–7
Picture Book 32, 80
Pied Piper of Hamlyn, The 62
Pingu 163
Planer, Nigel 66

Play Away 41, 71, 78, 145–7, *145*
Playbox 32, 80
Playdays 12, 49, 75, 76, 77, 78
Play School 37, 39–43, 46, 49, 65–6, 68–9, *69*, 70–1, 72–3, 74–8, 111, 124, 145–7, 162, 165
Pogles' Wood 62, *63*
Points of View 12
Portobello Productions 107
Postgate, Oliver 62, *63*
Postgate, Richmond 15, 19–20
Postman Pat 65
Press Gang 14, 102–3, *103*, 116
Preston, Trevor 94–5
Price to Play 144
Prix Jeunesse 44, 47, 105, 123
Puzzle Trail 151

Quayle, Nancy 69
Quest of Eagles 92

Radio 103
Radio Canada 165
Radio Roo 140
Radio Televisone Italiana 166
Radio Times 15, 20, 35, 156
Ragtime 71
Railway Children, The 23, *23*, 87
Rainbow 42, 47, 75–6, 115
Razzamatazz 144
Read, Mike 133
Really Wild Roadshow, The 119–20
Really Wild Show, The 119, *119*
Reay, Ann 71, 147, 167
Record Breakers 41, 147, *148*
Redmond, Phil 102–3
Reed, Owen 32, 34, 35–6, 42
Reith, (Lord) John 15
Reluctant Dragon, The 27
Rentaghost 152–3, *153*, 155
Ridsdale-Scott, Peter 71, 144
Rin Tin Tin 35
Ring-A-Ding 71
Roach, Jill 125, 126
Roberts, Bob *81*, 82
Robinson Crusoe 41
Robinson, Tony 86, 154
Rogers, Roy 34
Roland Rat 60, *61*
Rollings, Gordon 71
Romper Room 36, 42, 75
Round The Bend 60, *60*
Round the Twist 154, 165
Rowan, Eric 127, 129
Rowlands, Avril 124
Rubovia 52, *53*
Rudd, Lewis 46–7, 148, 167

Runaround 48, 151
Running Scared 101, 161
Rupert 67
Russell, Alan 148

Satellite Show, The 143
Saturday Picture Show 139
Saturday Special 33–4, 55
Saturday Superstore 115, 132, 133, 135, *138*, 140
Schofield, Phillip 26, 56, 133, *139*, 159–60
Search 115, 125
Secret Diary of Adrian Mole, aged 13¾, The 104
Secret Garden, The 9, 23, *24*, 32, 88
Secret World of Polly Flint, The 96–7, *97*
Secrets 105
See Saw 77
Sense of Guilt, A 102
Sesame Street 42–5, *43*, 58, 59, 74, 123
Seymour, Alan 94
S4C 67
Shadows 105
Shakespeare 67
Shang-a-lang 144
Silver Swan, The 87
Simon and the Witch 107, 152
Sims, Monica 37, *38*, 39, 41–3, 90
Singing Ringing Tree, The 41
Singleton, Valerie *110*, 111, 115, 160
Six O'Clock News 13
Sketch Club 122
Smike 105, *106*
Sooty 20, 50, 54–6, *56*, 65, 162
Sooty Show, The 55, *55*
Southern Television 47–8, 96, 103, 115, 150–1
Soyuzmutifilm 67
Spence, Penny 166
Spitting Image 60, 153
Splash 115
Spooky 105
Stephens, Doreen 36–8, *37*, 46, 66, 68
Stevens, Julie 71, *72*
Stingray 61
Stone, Paul 92, 94
Stories Round the World 105
Story Beneath the Sands, The 41, 116
Storyteller, The 58
Streatfeild, Noel 27, 91, 93, 101
Studio E 34, 79, 109
STV (Scottish Television) 140
Supercar 61
Supergran 153, *154*
Sutton, Shaun 34, 87, 101

S.W.A.L.K 104
Swan, Jeremy 105, 152
Swap Shop (see also *Multi-Coloured Swap Shop*) 130–1, 133, 158

Take Hart 41, 122
Talent Night 54
Talking Animal 120
Tarrant, Chris 134, *135*
Taylor, David 120
Teenage Mutant Hero (Ninja) Turtles 14, 67, 162
Telemagination 68
Telescope 20, 109
Television Is Good For Your Kids 85
Thames Television 11–12, 40, 46, 55, 64, 85, 95, 99, 104, 114, 117, 129, 148
Thief 105
Think Again 147, *148*
Think of a Number 41, 71, 147
Third Eye Productions 117
Thomas the Tank Engine 65
Thompson, Eric 66, *72*
Thompson Family, The 101
Thompson, Peter 18, 21
Three Scampis, The 144
3,2,1 Contact 117
Thrower, Percy 109–11
Thunderbirds 47, 61–2, *62*
Thundercats 67, 162
Thursday's Child 91
Tickertape 46
Tide Race 124
Tingha and Tucker Club, The 47, 56–7, 167
Tiswas 48, 130, 134, *135*, 136, 139, 151
Todd, Barbara Euphan 153
Toksvig, Sandi 136, *136*
Tom and Jerry 39, 41
Tomorrow People, The 47, 99, *100*, 101
Tom Tom 40, 115
Top of the Form 150, *150*

Toytown 16
Trace, Christopher *110*
Traveller in Time, A 113
Treasure Houses 117
Treasure Island 88
Treasure Seekers, The 32
Tree House Family, The 56
Trumpton 65
TSW (Television South West) 11
Tube, The 144
Tucker, Rex 18–19
Tucker's Luck 104, *104*
Turner, Sue 46, 113, 114–15, 137
TV (Television) Centre 51, 109, 140, 148
TV-am 60, 140
TV Ontario 165
TVS (Television South) 11, 67, 91, 93, 103, 105, 115, 120, 123–4, *135*–7
Tyne Tees Television 92, 105, 144
Uncle Jack 153, 155
Unsolved Mysteries 117

Val Meets the VIPs 115
Vanity Fair 89
Vice Versa 32
Vision On 40, *121*, 122

Wade, Laurence 115
Warden's Niece, The 90
Warner Brothers 140
Warren, Charles 76
Warrior Queen, The 47, 99, *99*
Watch With Mother 30, 36, 43, 49, 62, 69, 77
Water Trolley, The 166
Waterman, Dennis 107, 152
We Are The Champions 41, 71
We Are The Champions Special 123, *123*
We'll Tell You A Story 85
West Country Television 12
Westmore, Michael 18–19, 21
What's All This Then? 143

What's That Noise? 124
What's Up, Doc? 140
What's Your Story? 86
Wheldon, (Sir) Huw 25, *25*, 31, 33, 37–8, 42
When Santa Rode the Prairie 105
Whirligig 20, 33
Whitby, Joy 37, 46, 66, 68–9, 71, 75, 80, 124, 146
White Horses, The 41
White Peak Farm 101
Whitelaw, Billie 82, 107
Whoosh! 130
Why Bird (*Playdays*) 77
Wide Awake Club 140
Wildsmith, Brian 65
Wildtrack 118
Wilkinson, Barry 83
Williams, Kenneth 82, 83
Williams, Leila 110, *110*
Wilton, Nick 147
Wind in the Willows, The 62
Winners 165
Winnie-the-Pooh 83
Witch's Daughter, The 90, *91*
Wombles, The 64, *64*
Wood, Ann 60
Wood, Ivor 65
Wood, Wendy 82
Woodentops, The 49, 51
Woof 152, *152*
Worzel Gummidge 48, 96, 153
Write A Play 86
Wyatt, Will 160

Young, Muriel 144, 167
Young Person's Guides 105
Yorkshire Television 96, 124, 153

Z Shed 131
Zara Knows All 52
Zenith North 88
Zokko! 41, 130
Zoo Quest 34, 117
Zoo Time 47